# World War 1 The Canadian Response

William Henry Graham, M.S.Ed

# DEDICATION

I dedicate this humble offering to all those brave souls, who in August, 1914 committed to serve their country in the defense of England. Many of them leaving families and stable environments to face the unknown.

In my case I dedicate this to five cousins and one uncle who went overseas in the first war.

Two died and two of the three returning were awarded the Military Cross for being wounded at VIMY Ridge.

I hope that this book can be used as a resource for schools to increase the knowledge of our great Canadian contribution in lives and dollars to world freedom.
2nd. Printing December 27, 2020

Also, my sincere thanks to Shirley for help with editing

# CONTENTS

# ACKNOWLEDGMENTS

My information comes from years of searching government records, Wikipedia and personal family files.

# CHAPTER 1

# HOW WARS AND CONFLICTS START

## SOME CAUSES

Wars are generally caused by several factors, often happening over a period of months or years. The actions are often violent disputes. And often when war is declared both sides would be hard pressed to explain the exact cause or what was the tipping point.

**Religion** is often the cause of war as we have seen in Ireland and other countries. Muslims striving to have everyone follow their religion. The conflicts between the Protestants and Roman Catholics in the mid1850s. Religious wars go back for many centuries with many guilty parties.

**Revolutionary Wars** have been common throughout the world by changing the government with violent protests and actions. The American Revolution between the North and the South wanting to separate is a well-remembered example.

**Common Pact** in the case of many countries including Canada and Newfoundland and others supporting Britain during the First World War.

**Language and Nationalism** as we see in Canada between Quebec and other Provinces, and in many other places.

**Territorial Gains** in cases such as China wanting power and control over Taiwan. Or the government taking ownership of lands of the American Indians or Canadian Indians. Perhaps the Israeli/ Palestine conflict would also fit here, as well as other examples.

**Business** is often a cause of war with companies wanting to make armaments, electronics and all products used in the war machine.

Money and big business has substantial control over politicians and these decisions.

**Wealth and Resources** are a common cause of war when a country has rich mineral or oil reserves and other countries want these resources. Oil and other natural resources have always been a good reason to start a conflict, and still is.

**Nationalism** is often the cause of war in instances such as Scotland and Ireland wanted to be free of Britain and be their own independent nations. We could also include those in Quebec wanting to leave Canada or Alberta. Nationalism could also be caused by internal insurrection against a dictator.

**Greed** when a country simply wants what is not theirs and think they can increase their wealth by waging war. Perhaps this should be the more common cause.

**Many of these causes combine to cause war to be declared and people to die or be wounded - and for what reason.**

And each world war was the war to end all wars . . So we were told.

VIMY Ridge – Picture Courtesy Canada War Museum

# CHAPTER 2

# THE FIRST SIGNS OF WAR

**June 28th., 1914**, Archduke Franz Ferdinand heir to the Austria-Hungary throne and Sophie Ferdinand, Duchess of Hohenberg were assassinated in Sarajevo, Bosnia

The Archduke was in Sarajevo to inspect the Bosnian Imperial Armed Forces. Tensions were high between Austria/Hungary and this trip was a risk which they decided to take. The Serbian Black Hand group, without the authorization of their government planned to kill the Archduke and Duchess by bombing the car. The attempt was bungled as the intended conspirator lost his nerve. However, as they travelled in the official procession, Gavrilo Princip, a 19 yr. old Serbian nationalist shot them at point blank range, killing them both almost instantly.

Austria and Hungary blamed the Serbian government for the attack. Russia was the powerful ally of Serbia.

**On July 23rd., 1914**, Austria-Hungary, with the support of Germany, proposed arbitration as a means to settle their dispute.

**On July 25th**, Austria-Hungary several all diplomatic ties with Serbia and began to mobilize their troops and prepare for war.

**July 26, 1914**, Britain tried to organize an international conference with the hope to resolve the dispute between Austria-Hungary and Serbia. France, Russia and Italy agreed to participate but Germany refused.

Austria next asked that Germany would be on its side against Russia and its allies which included France and Great Britain.

**July 27th**. The German High Seas Fleet was recalled from Norway and posted to war bases.

**July 28th.** British Fleets were ordered to war bases.

**On July 28th.,** 1914, one month after the assassination Austria-Hungary declared war on Serbia and so began the conflict we now remember as the **First World War.**

**On July 30th.,** Austrian warships bombarded Belgrade, the Serbian capital and Tar orders the mobilization of the Russian army

**On July 31st, 1914,** Russia reacted to the Austrian attack on its ally Serbia and began full mobilization of Russian forces. Germany demanded that this mobilization stop but to no avail.

**On August 1st., 1914,** Germany declared war on Russia and Belgium and France began full mobilization of their forces.

**On August 2nd., 1914** Germany sent an ultimatum to Belgium demanding troop passage through Belgian territory.

**August 3rd., 1914,** Belgium refused the German request. Germany declares war on France and invaded Belgium which had been neutral to this point. Britain followed with an ultimatum for Germany to withdraw from Belgium. Germany rejected the British ultimatum.

**August 4th., 1914,** Great Britain, seeing no other alternative, declared war on Germany. All parts of the Dominion were bound by this decision of the British Empire which included, Canada, India, Australia, New Zealand and South Africa.

**August 4th., 1914,** the United States declared its neutrality. President Woodrow Wilson wanted to continue trading with Britain, it's allies and also Germany, having sold over 1.5 Billion dollars of goods during 1916.

When Germany attacked American shipping, sinking the Lusitania with a loss of 188 deaths as well as the Germans deciding to blockade the Atlantic and attempted to pressure Mexico to start a war with the US, agreeing to pay all costs, at this point, the US realized they had no choice but to support the allies against Germany. The United States Congress declared war on Germany on April 6th., 1917.

So, is it reasonable to say that the First World War was started between Austria-Hungary and Serbia as a result of a 19 year old Serbian nationalist's action?

And because of this action countries fought for more than four years resulting in about **37 million** lives lost, not to mention the millions of dollars wasted.

During the First World War over 65,000,000 troops were mobilized among all the countries involved. There were over 37,000,000 casualties among all the countries involved. This was a loss of 57% of forces.

Ask yourself where the world and Canada would be, had the First World War not happened. What a waste of lives and wealth.

Also, think about the timeline. Nobody stopped to negotiate. Rather each day had an immediate action. The lesson to us must be that people have to pause, take a breath and move ahead more cautiously.

Canadian mobilized forces totaled 424,000 with almost 236,000 casualties, about 56%.

# CHAPTER 3

## CANADA IS COMMITTED

As early as August 1st., 1914, Canada assured Britain that, in the event of war, they would make every sacrifice for the Empire, including sending troops overseas.

The H.M.C.S. Rainbow was made available for trade protection.

Banks were authorized to pay in notes instead of gold.

H.M.C.S. Niobe and Rainbow were placed at the disposal of the British Admiralty.

**On August 4th,** the German Chancellor says that "just for a scrap of paper Great Britain was going to make war on a kindred nation who desired nothing more than to be friends with her."   (As reported by the British Ambassador at Berlin.)

Great Britain declares war on Germany at 11p.m. on August 4th, 1914.

The Prime Minister of France states: "What is being attacked is the freedom of Europe of which France and her Allies are proud to be the defenders."

**On August 4th**, the following message was received from King George.

"I desire to express to my people of the Overseas Dominions with what appreciation and pride I have received the messages from their respective Governments during the past few days. These spontaneous assurances of their fullest support recalled to me the generous self-sacrificing help given by them in the past to the Mother Country. I shall be strengthened in the discharge of the great responsibilities which rest upon me by the confident belief that in this time of trial my Empire will stand united, calm, resolute, trusting in God. - George R.I."

The Naval Volunteer Force was placed on active service.

The Governor General to H.M. the King – "Canada stands united from the Pacific to the Atlantic in her determination to uphold the honour and tradition of our Empire."

**On August 5th., 1914**, a proclamation called Parliament together for a special War Session.

Authority was given to call out the Militia to complete the balance of 30 days training.

**Also on this same date**, the German minelayer SMS Konigin Luise was sunk by gunfire off Yarmouth, but not before she had laid a good many mines.

SS Konigin Luise
The First Casualty

Courtesy Wikipedia

**On August 6th.,** all Active Militia were called for active service and mobilization of volunteers for overseas was authorized. At the same time the Battles of the Frontiers began in the eastern frontiers of France and southern Belgium. These were five battles initiated by the French Commander Joseph Joffre. They were all lost to the German army. They were the first battled of the war.

**Also on this same date,** Serbia declares war on Germany and Austria-Hungary declares war on Russia.

**Also on this same date,** the naval convention between France and Great Britain concluded in London. A French Admiral was to command the Allied Naval forces in the Mediterranean.

**On August 6th.,** the first call for volunteers was issued.

**On August 7<sup>th</sup>.,** Canada purchased two submarines and put them at the Admiralty disposal. At the same time the first units of the British Expeditionary Force were landing in France.

**Also on this same date,** Ottawa decided that there would be a total of 25,000 troops. Additional lines were later added bringing the total to over 30,000.

**On August 8<sup>th</sup>.,** Hostilities had started in East Africa and in Togoland with the H.M.S. Amphion (pictured here) sunk by a mine off Yarmouth.

Amphion about 1914
Courtesy of Wikipedia

**Also on this same date,** Portugal declares herself an ally.

**On August 11th.,** the German warships Goeben and Breslau entered the Dardanelles which is a narrow strait between Turkey and the Gallipoli Peninsula.

**On August 12<sup>th</sup>.,** Great Britain and France declare war on Austria-Hungary.

**Also on this same date,** Commanding officers were to assemble all medically fit volunteers for the Overseas Expeditionary Force at local corps headquarters for instructional purposes. Commencing on August 12<sup>th</sup>., pay, field allowance and subsistence would be paid at the militia rates for active service – $1.00 per day for privates. Civil servants who might be called out would receive their regular par as well as the military emoluments. The Adjutant-General instructed that two Brigades would proceed to Camp Valcartier to prepare for the units of the force a camp staff of 17 officers and 63 other ranks.

The camp staff was actually formed on August 20<sup>th</sup>., with Colonel V.A.S. Williams named Camp Commandant.

**On August 13<sup>th</sup>.** Austrian forces crossed the river Drina and began an invasion of Serbia that ended on August 25<sup>th</sup>.

**Also on this same date,** four squadrons of The Royal Flying Corps flew from Dover to France. They were the first units to do this.

A division of the Canadian Postal Corps with vehicles and horses also arrived at Camp Valcartier.

**On August 14th.,** the battles of Morhange and Sarrebourg (North-Eastern France) began and ended on August 20th., 1914

**Also on this same date,** the Adjutant General urgently advised that all volunteers be inoculated for Typhoid with vaccine from the Ontario Board of Health and noted on each man's paper. An important restriction, removed a year later, was that no married man should enlist without the consent of his wife. The minister of Militia repeatedly insisted that service should be entirely voluntary.

**On August 15th.,** the Japanese government sent an ultimatum to Germany demanding evacuation of Tsingtau, China.

The first of the Dominion forces to go overseas was an expeditionary force, 1,383 strong, which sailed from Wellington, N.Z., on the 15th August 1914, under escort of three British, one French and two Australian warships, and formally hoisted the British flag on Samoa on 21st August.

A similar force, 1,500 strong, the Australian Naval and Military Expeditionary Force, began enlistment on 11th August and embarked a week later. Although delayed for a week awaiting escort, this force, supported by three cruisers, two destroyers and two submarines, all of the Royal Australian Navy, forced the capitulation of German New Guinea on 19th September.

**On August 16th.,** the landing of the original British Expeditionary Force, consisting of 4 Divisions and 1 Cavalry Division in France, was completed.

**On August 17th.,** the First Canadian Contingent was authorized and consisted of one Infantry Division and Army troops.

They later increased this by one Cavalry Brigade and other units . This and all later contingents were equipped and maintained at the expense of Canada.

**Also on this same date,** the Belgian Government transferred from Brussels to Antwerp.

**On August 18th.,** The Canadian Prime Minister Sir Robert Borden opened the session with the following:

"As to our duty, all are agreed; we stand shoulder to shoulder with Britain and the other British Dominions in this quarrel.
And that duty we shall not fail to fulfill as the honour of Canada demands."

**As of August 18th.,** the volunteers for the C.E.F. (Canadian Expeditionary Force) numbered 26,250

| Area | Officers | Other ranks |
|---|---|---|
| 1st Div. Area Western Ontario | 78 | 1,696 |
| 2nd Div. Area Central Ontario | 281 | 5,618 |
| 3rd Div. Area Eastern Ontario | 120 | 1,850 |
| 4th Div. Area Quebec HQ Montreal | 153 | 3,290 |
| 5th Div. Area Eastern Quebec-Quebec | 31 | 537 |
| 6th Div. Area Maritime Prove – Halifax | 107 | 1,448 |
| M.D.#10 Manitoba & Saskatchewan | 254 | 5,322 |
| M.D.#11 B.C and Yukon – Victoria | 284 | 3,033 |
| M.D.#13 Alberta – Calgary | 127 | 1966 |
| Other Details | | 55 |
| **TOTAL** | **1,435** | **24,815** |

**NOTE**: The Canadian Parliament didn't choose to go to war in 1914. The country's foreign affairs were guided in London. So when Britain's ultimatum to Germany to withdraw its army from Belgium expired on 4 August 1914, the entire British Empire, including Canada, was at war, allied with Serbia, Russia, and France against the German and Austro-Hungarian empires

**On August 19th.,** The term of the Governor General, the Duke of Connaught, was extended for the duration of the war.

**Also on this same date,** the Battle of Gawaiten-Gumbinnen (East Prussia) happened and lasted 1 day.

**On August 20th.,** German forces occupied Brussels (Belgium).

**On August 21st.,** German forces attacked Namur in Belgium and captured it four days later. German forces also captured Charleroi, Belgium on August 24th.

**Also on this same date,** the British Government issued orders to raise the first new army of six divisions.

**On August 22, 1914**, a Special War Session of Parliament prorogued and passed:

- War Appropriations Act, 1914 included the following:
- Authorizing payment of $50,000,000 for war purposes.
- Making of regulations for the security and welfare of Canada.
- Confirming financial measures already taken and providing for moratorium.
- Assisting families of Canadians on active service.

**On August 22nd.** There were 20,089 troops at Valcartier (Quebec) and by the 8th of September the maximum number of 32,665 had been reached. In the final outcome, the total number enlisted for the first contingent was 36,000.

**Also on this same date,** Austria-Hungary declared war on Belgium, although for reasons unknown it was only received by Belgium on August 28th.

**Note:**
With almost two million men of military age in Canada, an average of nearly fifty thousand had trained annually with the Canadian Militia in the previous five years, so Canada had considerable training and experience to offer.

There is no exact record of the total number of volunteers for overseas service. Many were rejected at recruiting offices on physical grounds; others were refused enlistment at Valcartier for a multitude of other reasons, including not having permission of their wives. However, the total number enlisted in the first contingent was about **36,000.**

Three provinces furnished less than the quota allotted in the Overseas Expeditionary Force original plan of 1911-12, while Ontario, for whatever reason, furnished almost seven times that Quota, supplying  more than one-third of the whole contingent, while six provinces, for whatever reason, sent fewer than trained with the Militia in 1913-1914. A few Indians (First Nations) were enlisted, including three descendants of Joseph Brant. Colored volunteers were refused, as racism was alive and healthy at the time.

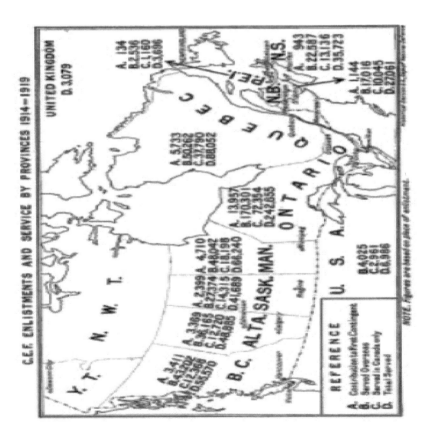

Great Britain's declaration of war automatically committed Newfoundland to the struggle, but the dominion government's patriotic response was genuine and popularly shared.

Newfoundland doubled the numbers of its branch of the Royal Naval Reserve and sent a body of men to take part in the operations at the front.

Of the 1,500 officers, two thirds were Canadian born and twenty-nine percent were other, mainly British. They had all undergone training in the Canadian Militia and qualified for their ranks in Canadian military schools, including 121 from the Royal Military College in Kingston.

Of the 34,500 rank and file, less than 30% were Canadian-born with sixty-five percent born in the British Isles or other British possessions. 26% were born in the United States.

While some had served in other forces, the most were men without training or experience. All volunteers were attested (sworn in) by a magistrate or Justice of Peace for the Province of Quebec, with the following oath.

**"I………..do sincerely promise and swear (or solemnly declare) that I will be faithful and bear true allegiance to His Majesty."**

Regardless of this oath being taken, all ranks at Valcartier had to also subscribe to this additional oath administered by a Justice of the Peace.

**"I…………..do make oath, that I will be faithful and bear true allegiance to His Majesty King George the Fifth, His Heirs and Successors. And that I will as in duty bound honestly and faithfully defend His Majesty, His Heirs and Successors, in Person, Crown and Dignity, against all enemies, and will observe and obey all Orders of His Majesty, His Heirs and Successors, and of all the Generals and Officers set over me. So help me God."**

## COMMITMENT OF EACH PROVINCE AND DOMINION

➤ 1,000,000  Bags of flour from the Dominion
➤ 500,000 bushels of Oats from Alberta
➤ 100,000  tons of Coal from Nova Scotia
➤ 4,000,000 pounds of Cheese from Quebec
➤ 100,000 bushels of Oats from Prince Edward Island
➤ 100,000 bushels of Potatoes from New Brunswick
➤ $500,000 in Money and 250,000 bags of flour from Ontario
➤ 50,000 bags of flour from Manitoba
➤ 1,500 Horses from Saskatchewan
➤ 25,000 cases of canned Salmon

The British Government, in accepting with gratitude these timely gifts, stated that the horses would be of great assistance to them in mounting cavalry and yeomanry regiments, and the supplies would be used for the relief of stress.

## Valcartier Camp

In 1912, the Minister of the Militia took an option on 4,391 acres of land along the Canadian Northern Railway, about 16 miles northwest of Quebec City. The camp was 12,428 acres at a final cost of $428,131.00.

The Militia purchased the property and $10,000.00 to $15,000.00 for camp construction which included a water supply, rifle ranges, etc.
Two separate telephone lines were installed from the camp to Quebec City. The total cost of all construction to complete Camp Valcartier was $185,436.50.

The intended use of the camp was for concentration, organization and training of the Canadian Expeditionary Force of 25,000.

The camp staff was formed on August 20th with Colonel V.A.S. Williams named Camp Commandant. Forty cadets were attached—each with his own bicycle – for duty as dispatch riders.

**On August 23<sup>rd</sup>.,** other things were happening in Europe as the battle of Tannensberg (East Prussia) began and continued until August 31<sup>st</sup>., 1914. At the same time countries continued to take sides.

**On that same date**, the British and German troops engaged at Mons (Belgium) as the British tried to slow the German advance. The recapture of Mons was one of the final battles of the war happening on the 9<sup>th</sup> to 11<sup>th</sup> of November, 1918. Canadians can rightly be proud of their actions in the final battle of Mons as they freed Mons and almost 800 French civilians, under the leadership of General Curry.

**On August 24<sup>th</sup>.,** the first units of the Indian Expeditionary force left India for France.

**On August 25<sup>th</sup>.,** Japan declared war on Austria-Hungary.

**On that same date**, the first use of British aircraft for patrol purposes over the retreating British forces in France.

**On August 26<sup>th</sup>.,** 1914 the Battle of Le Cateau (Northern France) took place and Longwy capitulated to German forces. Louvain was sacked and Noyon, Cambrai and Douai were occupied by German Forces. They were retaken on the 9<sup>th</sup> and 17<sup>th</sup> of October in 1918.

The first Battle of Lemberg (Galicia) began on this date and ended on August 30<sup>th</sup>., 1914.

The Battle of Zomosc-Komarow (Russian – Poland) began and ended on Sept 2<sup>nd</sup>., 1914. The German forces in Togoland capitulate to Allied Forces.

**On August 27<sup>th</sup>.** The British marines landed at Ostend (Flemish Region of Belgium).

**On August 28<sup>th</sup>.,** there was naval action off Heligoland (a German archipelago in the North Sea.)

**On August 29ᵗʰ.,** the First Battle of Guise (Northern France) begins and ends the following day. Arras (Northern France) was evacuated by French forces but re-occupied September 13ᵗʰ., 1914.

**On August 30ᵗʰ.,** Samoa (Germany controlled) was occupied, unopposed, by the New Zealand Expeditionary Force.

**On August 31ˢᵗ.,** Amiens (Northern France) was entered by German forces but re-occupied on September 13ᵗʰ., 1914.

**On September 2ⁿᵈ.,** Japanese forces landed in Shantung (China) to attack Tsingtau (German port in China) which capitulated on November 7ᵗʰ., 1914.

**On that same date,** the French Government transferred from Paris to Bordeaux. * Transferred back the 18ᵗʰ of November.

**On September 3ʳᵈ.,** Lemberg (Galacia) was captured by Russian forces.

**On September 4ᵗʰ.,** the Battle of Grand Couronne (Nancy) began and ended on September 12ᵗʰ.

**On September 5ᵗʰ.,** the retreat from Mons ended and the Battle of Ourcq began.

The German forces had reached Clays, 10 miles from Paris which was their nearest point during the war.

The Battle of Masurian Lakes (East Prussia) began and ended 10 days later.

The German forces crossed the frontier of Northern Rhodesis.

**On that same date,** the British, French and Russian governments signed the "Pact of London" agreeing not to make separate peace.

**On September 6ᵗʰ.**, the Battle of Marne (Franve) began and ended four days later with the Germans starting to retreat on September 9ᵗʰ., 1914.

**On September 8ᵗʰ., 1914,** Austrian forces began the second invasion of Serbia and ended on December 15ᵗʰ.

The Battle of Drina (Serbia) began on this date and ended September 17ᵗʰ.

The Second Battle of Lemberg (Galicia) began on this date and ended on September 11ᵗʰ.

**On September 11ᵗʰ.**, Austrian forces in Galicia retreated.

**On that same date**, the British Government issues orders to raise a second new army of six divisions.

An Australian Expeditionary Force landed on the Bismarck Archipelago (German New Guinea).

**On September 12ᵗʰ.**, the battle of Aisne (close to Paris) begins and lasted three days.

**On September 13ᵗʰ.**, the British Government issues orders to raise a third new army of six divisions.

**On September 15ᵗʰ.**, the Rebellion in South Africa begins.
On the same date, Trenches were first dug on the Western front

**On September 17ᵗʰ.**, the German New Guinea and surrounding colonies capitulate to the Australian Expeditionary Force.

**On September 22ⁿᵈ.**, the First Battle of Picardy (France) began and ended on September 26ᵗʰ.

**On September 24ᵗʰ.**, Peronne (France) was taken by German Forces and retaken March 18ᵗʰ., 1917.

On **September 26th**., Bapaume (France) was occupied by the Germans and retaken on March 17th., 1917

On **September 27th**., The First Battle of Artois (Northern France) begins and ends on October 12th. 1914.

## ALLIED POWERS

| Country | Total mobilized forces | Total casualties |
| --- | --- | --- |
| Russia | 12,000,000 | 9,150,000 |
| British Empire | 8, 904,467 | 3,190,235 |
| France | 8,410,000 | 6,160,800 |
| Italy | 5,615,000 | 2,197,000 |
| United States | 4,734,991 | 320,518 |
| Japan | 800,000 | 1210 |
| Romania | 750,000 | 535,706 |
| Serbia | 707,343 | 331,106 |
| Canada | 424,000 | 235,494 |
| Belgium | 267,000 | 93,061 |
| Greece | 230,000 | 27,000 |
| Portugal | 100,000 | 33,291 |
| Montenegro | 50,000 | 20,000 |
| **TOTALS** | **42,612,810** | **22,165,291** |

# CENTRAL POWERS

| | | |
|---|---|---|
| Germany | 11,000,000 | 7,142,558 |
| Austria-Hungary | 7,800,000 | 7,020,000 |
| Turkey | 2,850,000 | 975,000 |
| Bulgaria | 1,200,000 | 266,919 |
| **TOTALS** | **22,850,000** | **15,404,477** |
| **GRAND TOTALS** | **65,462,810** | **37,569,768** |

| | | |
|---|---|---|
| **Total Killed** | = | **8,598,009** |
| **Total Wounded** | = | **21,390,000** |
| **Prisoners or Missing** | = | **7,754,700** |

## World War 1 included almost 100 countries.

- ➢ The Americas, Australasia, Europe, Africa and Asia.
- ➢ Over 2 million Africans served as soldiers and laborers.
- ➢ Of Asian countries, India sent the most with over 1.2 million troops.
- ➢ China wanted to stay neutral but over 200,000 laborers worked for the Allied Forces repairing tanks.
- ➢ Japan sent 14 destroyers to assist the British.
- ➢ Australia, a British colony at the time contributed over 330,000 soldiers at the onset of the battles.
- ➢ Almost 8 million French citizens served in the first war.

## It was indeed a "World War" with almost all of the world involved in some way.

# CHAPTER 4

# ON THE HOME FRONT

**On the home front – things were also happening.**

**On September 8th., 1914** a Shell Committee was appointed by the Minister of Militia.    A Colonel (hon.) Cantly was one of the members.  Col Cantly started with the steel industry in New Glasgow, NS, was in charge of the Wabana, Iron Ore mines in Newfoundland, In charge of Steel operations in North Sydney, Nova Scotia and invented the steel finally used in the shells.

**On that same date**, 32,449 of all ranks were on parade at Valcartier Camp.

**On September 9th., 1914**, the Royal Canadian Regiment sailed from Halifax under escort of  H.M.C.S. Niobe, to relieve the 2nd Battalion, Lincolnshire Regiment on Garrison duty, in Bermuda.

**On September 20th.,** the Prime Minister Bordon therefore decided on 20th September to despatch to England the entire force under arms at Valcartier, and announced that the decision had been reached because the Cabinet deemed it advisable that the force should be continually kept at full strength by readily available reinforcements.

A large amount of equipment was purchased in the United States including Colt automatic machine guns, armoured cars, trucks and automobiles.

Even before the decision was taken that a contingent should be sent overseas, tabulated lists were compiled—by direction of the Camp Quartermaster-General—of the equipment and clothing required for 30,000, and for the supply of stores, vehicles, harness and saddlery.

The stores on hand were totally inadequate; the strength of the Contingent was increased, and troops on home defence must be provided for; the first contracts were therefore let to supply clothing for 50,000 troops, of date 10th August, with completion of delivery by 21st September. Such large orders meant that, in the case of clothing, the wool had to be procured and woven before the articles could be made up; and at least ten days must elapse, while leather was being procured, before manufacture of boots could begin.

This was the first of a series of requisitions approved by the Minister, without reference to Privy Council for authority. He saw that the short time allowable for deliveries, which must be completed before the Contingent could sail, made it absolutely imperative that all orders should be placed at the earliest possible moment.

Other batches of requisitions were passed, as quickly as they could be prepared by the Q.M.G's staff, for corresponding quantities of hardware, cutlery, harness, saddlery, and leather goods of all kinds, drugs, surgical supplies, electrical supplies, canvas goods, cotton and linen goods, knit goods and blankets. Certain of these were supplied under existing contracts for the Militia, but more were required, and all for delivery by 21st September at latest.

Some items were specially made on short notice such as: An unusual article of equipment, which might be classed as armament, was a special type of combination shovel designated "MacAdam," because recently patented by the Minister's lady secretary, and sponsored by him. It was made of 3/16" metal said to be capable of stopping a bullet at 300 yards, the blade was 8½" by 9¾" long, with a loophole 3¼" by 2" in one upper quarter, the handle, integral with the blade, was 4" long, and the weight was 5 lbs. 4 ozs; the infantryman was to use it either for digging or as a shield. This was rejected by the British, however, It might have been useful for the Tunnelers.

Aside from vehicles, motorcycles and bicycles horses were also required. 7,264 riding, artillery and draught horses, described as "sound in wind and limb and free from all blemishes." Their colour might be bay, brown, black, chestnut, blue roan or red roan; ages must be between five and eight years and heights from 15 to 16 hands, weight 1,000 to 1,400 lbs., dependent upon category. The price must average $175, and that sum was paid to any officer who wished to bring his own charger, provided it met the above requirements.

In all cases a Veterinary Officer, or a civil veterinary surgeon paid at the rate of $10 per day, was required to pass upon fitness and to countersign the cheque.

The purchasing agents quickly secured a number of horses and began shipping them as early as 20th August to Valcartier. After culling the group there were about 7,600 horses fit for service.

**On September 22nd. And 23rd.,** marked the beginning of the embarkation of the  C.E.F. (Canadian Expeditionary Force) at Quebec.

## PAY AND ALLOWANCES

Officers and Nursing Sisters were granted $50.00 towards expenses of outfit. This was later increased by $100.00.

Pay ranged from $20.00 per diem for a Major-General to $5.00 for a Lieut.-Colonel to $1.00 for gunners, sappers, drivers and privates.

Field allowance ranged from $4.00 per diem to ten cents.

Officers in command of over 500 troops received an additional $1.00 per day.

Working pay for non-commissioned officers and men enlisted as farriers, cooks, bakers, shoeing smiths, saddlers, wheelers, butchers, cooks, motor car drivers, received, according to classification   50 cents, 75 cents and $1.00 per diem.

All ranks could not assign more than four-fifths of their pay to relatives.

To provide for wives and families of  soldiers absent on duty a monthly separation allowance of $20.00 was granted to the rank and file, scaling upwards to $60.00 for Colonels.

Pensions for soldiers totally disabled on active service ranged from $150.00 for privates to $1,200 for a lieutenant-colonel. These rates were all eventually increased with allowances for each child.

**On October 1st.,** Colonel J.W. Carson, agent of the Minister of Militia in the United Kingdom established his office in London.

**Newfoundland**, a separate British dominion in 1914 and not yet a province of Canada, contributed 12,000 military personnel to Allied forces from a pre-war population of 242,000.

Newfoundland had a high fatality rate of over 1,200 with over 2,200 wounded.

The **Princess Patricia's Canadian Light Infantry** (P.P.C.L.I. or "Princess Pats") was the first Canadian fighting unit to go to France. It joined the 27th British Division, and would not become a part of the Canadian Forces until a year later.

# CHAPTER 5

# ARRANGING TRANSPORT

In the preliminary negotiations to hire transports to carry the First Contingent to Europe the Minister took direct action. As a result of the War Office enquiry, he called representatives of the large shipping companies to meet him at Ottawa on 15th August, explaining to them that bottoms would be required to transport a military force of about 25,000 troops from Quebec across the Atlantic before the middle of September.

The Q.M.G. Branch selected suitable ships from those which the companies reported could be made available, and by 11th September contracts, approved by the Department of Justice, had been signed by the Deputy Minister of Militia for twenty ships, of which nine were primarily and two partly for horses.

The inclusion of extra Line of Communication units needed four more vessels, and the decision to send the whole force assembled at Valcartier an additional six, the last of which was engaged at the last moment. Vessels were chartered at the Admiralty rates based on speed; per month, of which ten shillings was paid in advance.

In the charter-party, provision was made that when ships carried private cargo, as was permitted, any money derived from this source was to be credited to the Canadian Government, which assumed all war risks on hull, cargo and freight.

Rationing on approved menus was undertaken by the steamship companies at a fixed rate of $1.10 per diem for officers warrant officers and sergeants, and .65c for other ranks. A guarantee was also given that an extra supply of provisions to provide a margin of safety of seven days, over the estimated fourteen, would be carried.

Staff officers found that some of the fourteen chartered ships there assembled had been loaded to the hatches with private freight and 135,275 bags of the gift flour for the Mother Country.

To make space for military vehicles and baggage some were partly unloaded, a proceeding which changed the capacity figures. The motor
Trucks for the Supply Column and the Divisional Ammunition Park were too large for the hatchways of all but one ship—the *Manhattan*.

Some ships were short of furnishings and the Department of Militia and Defence had to loan 2,855 beds, also bedding, enamelled ware, camp stools and even lifebelts. Discussions arose over the number of officers per cabin and the number of horses per attendant—military regulations prescribed four horses, civil twenty; in the end, owing to lack of passenger accommodation in some of the horse ships, the maximum was sixteen.

It had been intended that the horse ships, being slower, should be filled first and despatched in advance on 24th September, under escort of H.M.C.S. *Niobe,* but it was found that they could not all be ready before 27th September,125 so it was decided that they would accompany the troopships,  and the loading of mounted and dismounted units proceeded simultaneously.

At Quebec were also loaded guns, stores and ammunition consigned to the D.D.O.S., Woolwich, the major items of which were forty-two 18-pdr. guns, nine 13-pdr., six 60- pdr., fifty-six ammunition wagons and 11,847 rounds of gun ammunition, as a contribution to the common stock from Canada's reserve supplies.

These were in excess of the fifty-four 18-pdr. guns, twelve 13-pdr. and four 60-pdr., with their full complement of 198 ammunition wagons, and 1,500 rounds per gun, which were required for mobilization of the artillery units of the Contingent.

Command of the Contingent was vested in Colonel V. A. S. Williams, the senior military officer present. He and the headquarters staff of the Contingent all embarked in the *Franconia*.

After loading, transports anchored in the stream where sealed orders were handed to the captain of the ship and to the commander of the troops on board.

The first of these, issued by the Chief Transportation Officer, directed the captain to proceed down river; the second, from the same source and opened after dropping the pilot off Father Point, was to continue the voyage to Gaspé Basin, at the entrance to which the Canadian Government ship *Canada* would
transmit orders for anchorage. The third was a farewell message read to the troops assembled on deck:–

F.M. Arthur, Governor General of Canada stated: "On the eve of your departure from Canada I wish to congratulate you on having the privilege of taking part, with the other forces of the Crown, in fighting for the honour of the King and Empire.

You have nobly responded to the call of duty, and Canada will know how to appreciate the patriotic spirit that animates you.

I have complete confidence that you will do your duty, and that Canada will have every reason to be proud of you. You leave these shores with the knowledge that all Canadian hearts beat for you, and that our prayers and best wishes will ever attend you. May God bless you and bring you back victorious."

The Department of the Naval Service had been requested to ensure " that every possible precaution be taken to detect and prevent the laying of mines in the St. Lawrence, or elsewhere on the route to England": neither had equipment for mine-sweeping, but both issued warnings that careful watch should be kept for mines or suspicious vessels in the river – they did not accept responsibility for the remainder of the route.

Before leaving Quebec strict injunctions had been issued in secret orders to captains of vessels from Rear- Admiral R. E. Wemyss,
For the covering of lights, which were observed, and for the
closing down of ships' wireless, which were not always observed at first.

The press had been warned against giving the names of the ships or making mention of the embarkation of the force.

This was complied with by almost all Canadian newspapers, but soon the information was broadcast to the world at large. On 28th September, in the very midst of the embarkation, the Governor General was reported in the press to have stated at a public meeting in Ottawa:– Recently I have had the pleasure several times to visit Valcartier, and also to be present at what is perhaps no longer a secret, the embarkation of the Canadian troops.

On the same occasion the Prime Minister is reported to have said:– Twice I have visited Valcartier Camp. Those of you who have not had that opportunity may be assured that the expeditionary force which has just embarked comprises as splendid a body of men as will be found among the armies of the Empire.

These pronouncements were calculated to deceive the enemy and, to further the deception, Admiral Wemyss let the press understand that the transports were sailing independently.

The War Office was scrupulous to encipher all cables, and had pressed for details of personnel, horses and material in each transport; the list was so extensive that the department warned the War Office that it would be sent in clear, and so despatched it. The warning cable drew remonstrances from the War Office, and the reply given was: "Your telegram received too late," and on the same day: "Unlikely to do harm . . . . Names of transport and strength of Contingent had already been published." As it happened no harm was done, and although even newspapers with ample information undoubtedly reached Germany before the convoy made port, no effectual interceptive action was taken by the German Admiralty; it is now known that Admiral von Tirpitz believed 20,000 Canadians to be in Le Havre on 8th October.

Guarding the western entrance to the English Channel, in co-operation with a French squadron, was the 12th Cruiser Squadron commanded by Rear-Admiral R. E. Wemyss. On 10th September he was ordered to hand over to Admiral Bethell, commanding the 7th Battle Squadron, and to proceed with his squadron to coal at Plymouth, and thence to Halifax to escort the Canadian convoy, then estimated at fourteen transports and expected to sail on the 24th.

Possible interference with the convoy might come from German warships based on home ports; or from the fourteen armed German liners in harbour at New York and Boston; or from the *Karlsruhe* in the Pernambuco area.

It was arranged that the British Grand Fleet should cover the first of these; Admiral Hornby with a cruiser squadron including the *Niobe,* would cover North American Atlantic ports; the escort would deal with immediate attacks. When it became known that the convoy would consist of thirty-two instead of fourteen transports, other powerful warships were detailed to accompany it.

The Minister was concerned for the safety of the convoy and enquired on 16th September as to the strength of the escort, pointing out the danger of capture arising from the varying speeds of the transports. The information sought was conveyed, three days later, to the Canadian Government as follows:–

The escort for the Canadian Contingent will consist of four cruisers with H.M.C.S. *Niobe* and H.M.S. *Glory,* under the command of a flag officer. This will be reinforced en route by a second battleship of the *Glory* class. The whole of the Grand Fleet will cover the escort from attack by any of the large forces of the enemy. All arrangements are being made by the Admiralty for the escort, and the safe conduct of the convoy is receiving the most careful consideration.

On September 15th, Admiral Wemyss was three days out of Plymouth, a cipher message informed the Minister of Militia that the cruisers would assemble in good time and that the Admiral would arrange direct with him the exact time and position at which his squadron would meet the convoy. Although a stiff head wind reduced the speed of the twenty-year old warships – *Charybdis* (flagship*), Eclipse* and *Talbot* – to ten knots, with the *Diana,* delayed at Plymouth by machinery defects, 300 miles behind, the squadron arrived at Halifax on 22nd September and the Admiral interviewed the Minister at Quebec on the 24th., and discovered that the convoy would consist **of thirty transports**, and changed his plans, to meet the increased number.

The next day he reported to the Admiralty that he would not be able to leave the St. Lawrence till 1st October. In accordance with his instructions troopships on arrival in Gaspé Basin were directed to anchor in the position each would occupy in the convoy when proceeding to sea in fleet formation; three lines ahead, fifteen cables apart and designated, **X, Y, Z,** each headed by a cruiser, with the fourth in rear.

| Z | Y | X |
|---|---|---|
| **H.M.S. ECLIPSE** | **H.M.S. DIANA** | **H.M.S. CHARYBDIS** |
| MEGANTIC | CARIBBEAN | SCOTIAN |
| RUTHENIA | ATHENIA | ARCADIAN |
| BERMUDIAN | ROYAL EDWARD | ZEELAND |
| ALAUNIA | FRANCONIA | CORINTHIAN |
| IVERNIA | CANADA | VIRGINIAN |
| SCANDINAVIAN | MONMOUTH | ANDANIA |
| SICILIAN | MANITOU | SAXONIA |
| MONTEZUMA | TYROLIA | GRAMPIAN |
| LAPLAND | TUNISIAN | LAKONIA |
| CASSANDRA | LAURENTIC | MONTREAL |
| ROYAL GEORGE | | |

But there were further delays and the flotilla did not sail on the 1st, or on the 2nd, on which day the Minister paid a visit to the Contingent in Gaspé Basin and passed in a launch from ship to ship distributing bundles of his printed valediction to the troops who received it with mixed feelings. On seeing the archaic cruiser escort he telegraphed to Ottawa a message for the Admiralty:–

"Escort altogether inadequate, should increase strength." The Governor General, in forwarding the message, enquired whether the Admiralty was thoroughly assured of the adequacy of the escort. The reply, which reiterated the previous explanation of the intended disposition of protective warships, was in the affirmative. But Admiral Wemyss had similar misgivings, and informed the Admiralty after the voyage that under the circumstances he considered the risks taken were unjustifiable.

**Let me digress slightly -**

## One nursing sisters description in her own words:

With the following words: "You have been selected as a Nursing-Sister for service abroad. You will report to Quebec on August 23rd. and mobilization. At this point we passed into the military machine indefinitely."

Sept 23rd found us assembled at Quebec. By that time, Camp Valcartier was completing training and equipment and ships were assembling in the harbour.

The Nursing-Sisters were under the command of Matron Margaret MacDonald of Brierly Brook, Nova Scotia.

Nurses were billeted in the Immigration Hospital on the outskirts of Quebec City. The building was filled with three tier wire bunks and the nurses bundled in military blankets and their nursing cloaks. As they were on the main road to Valcartier, with traffic continuing all night, there was very little sleep.

This heralded the weird but wonderful beginning of what would continue for the next four years in France and Flanders and other famous fields.

Canadian Nursing-Sisters describe themselves as being well billeted during the war, sometimes in hotels and usually having army beds rather than Camp cots to sleep on. Usually the food was good and whatever comforts they could get, usually due to their own initiatives.

The English army nurses noted how the Canadian nurses made their surroundings home like and suggested the Canadian nurses didn't know the war was on. However, the Canadian Nurses performance was considered beyond reproach.

At last the notice board bore the words:
"Sisters will prepare to embark at once"

# CHAPTER 6

## EMBARKATION AT LAST

At 2.30 p.m. on Saturday the 3rd October the flagship *Charybdis* signalled all transports:—

Have cables hove short. All ships in Column Z will raise anchors at 3 p.m. and proceed, keeping column formation, steaming at 9 knots following leading cruiser *Eclipse*.

Exactly at 3 p.m. the *Eclipse* led the port column out into the Gulf through the narrow exit from Gaspé Basin. As the last ship in Column Z passed the leading cruiser *Diana* of Column Y, all ships of that column hove anchors off bottom and proceeded, also at 9 knots, and similarly as the last transport of Column Y passed the leading cruiser *Charybdis* of Column X that column followed, with H.M.S. *Talbot* as Rear Cruiser. The length of the whole in line astern was about **21½ land miles**, and the last ships passed the entrance at about 6.00 p.m. As soon as the first column was out at sea, speed was reduced and the two other columns drew abreast in fleet formation.

Then the course for all ships was signalled, with the speed—10 knots—and the convoy proceeded on the first leg of the course of 2,504 miles to its final destination. By noon on Sunday the convoy was off Cape Ray. At 6.30 a.m. next day, off St. Pierre- Miquelon, the battleship *Glory*, from Admiral Hornby's squadron, joined the escort and took station five miles to the south; below the horizon and guarding the southern flank of the route was his flagship, the *Lancaster*, while the *Suffolk*, *Niobe*, and auxiliary cruiser *Caronia* watched the New York area.

In the middle of the forenoon four short quick blasts from the *Royal Edward*, which suddenly swung out of line, flying the flag signal "Man Overboard," were noted by the next ship astern, the *Franconia*. In answer to the whistle signal the *Franconia* reversed engines to full speed astern, while from the bridge a ready lifebuoy was thrown within a few yards of the man in passing.

Meanwhile a boat, the crew in their places, was lowered and dropped in ninety seconds and the man was picked up safely. The boat recovered, the transports resumed their places.

At 11.00 a.m. the transport *Florizel*, with the Newfoundland Contingent on board, joined the convoy and took station as the last transport in the northern column. In the afternoon a strange steamer was chased by the cruiser *Eclipse* and found to be harmless.

The routine on board the transports was left to the commander of the troops in consultation with the captain of the ship. Reveille as a rule was at 5.30 or 6.30 a.m., followed by physical exercises and breakfast from 7.00 to 8.00 a.m. The forenoon was occupied with sweeping, cleaning, guard mounting and morning parades. The hour of the midday meal varied from 11.45 a.m. to 1.00 p.m., after which the afternoon parade was held. Morning and afternoon parades included rifle exercise, squad and section drill, signalling, physical exercises and fire drill.

On all ships boat drill was carried out at least twice during the voyage and several muster parades were held; on Sundays there were church parades, and on Saturday sports. Lectures for officers were delivered at 5.00 p.m. and 8.00 p.m.; tea for the men was at 6.00 p.m.; dinner for the officers at 7.00 p.m., and although "Lights Out" was sounded at 9.15 p.m. time was found in almost every ship for concerts, when local talent provided entertainment, and the usual collection was made for seamen's charities.

The daily run—from 200 to 250 miles— and the noon position aroused the usual interest, and although the sending of wireless by the transports was forbidden "except in the case of dire necessity," news of the outside world was picked up by wireless from passing vessels or from the Marconi station at Poldhu (South Cornwall, England).

On October 5th. the Newfoundland contingent in the ship Florizel joined the convoy off Cape Race (Newfoundland – Avalon Peninsula).

Strange steamers were sighted on the 6th and 7th.

The two fast transports *Laurentic* and *Royal George* acted as scouts on either flank during the hours of daylight. At midday on the 8th, Admiral Hornby's flagship *Lancaster* steamed through the convoy from east to west between Columns X and Y, signalling "Good Luck" on leaving the escort at longitude 40° W.—the eastern limit of his station.

No lights of any kind, except an oil steering light on the stern of each vessel. Probably an additional small oil lamp in the wheel house lighting the compass.

At daylight on Saturday, 10th October at 49° 45' N.— 27° 05' W. two large ships were sighted ahead; these were the *Princess Royal* and *Majestic* which had been waiting at this rendezvous for two days. The former, a battle cruiser from the Grand Fleet, took up position on the north wing about six miles distant; the latter, a battleship from Admiral Bethell's squadron, took station about six miles ahead of the centre column, and both kept position with the convoy.

Next day, as an advance squadron, the *Alaunia* and *Montreal* were sent ahead, following the *Diana,* which was replaced by the *Majestic* at the head of Y Column.

The 12th of October was a memorable day as the Princess Royal visited the convoy in late afternoon as a red sun was setting in a smooth sea. She left her position, steamed back to the rear of the convoy and then, cleared for action and dressed as for a review, thundered up the line at 22 knots between Y and Z Columns. Passing the transports the band played "O Canada" and "The Maple Leaf," the officers stood on the quarter-deck, the crew gave three cheers, and the crowding troops responded lustily to the welcome.

On the same day the Admiral sent a warning order that next day (Tuesday 13th of October) the transports would be organized into three squadrons – White (12 knots), Blue (10 knots), and Red (8 knots). But next morning the flagship signalled "All ships will keep present fleet formation till further advised."

A northerly gale had sprung up during the night, there was a heavy sea, and the flagship at 8.00 a.m. had picked up strong German wireless telegraph signals, which even yet are not definitely accounted for: on the same day a German submarine was reported off Cherbourg (Northwestern France), and another near Culver (Isle of Wight) narrowly escaped being rammed by the British torpedo-boat,

The presence of the submarines caused the Admiralty to change the destination of the convoy.

The original idea had been that the Contingent should disembark at Liverpool; this was abandoned because of congestion in the Mersey, and the War Office made plans to take the troops by rail from Southampton to camps on Salisbury Plain; German activity in the Channel had caused a change to Devonport on 30th September; but on account of War Office objection Southampton was again agreed upon on 10th October, and Admiral Wemyss had been so informed.

At 6.30 p.m. on the 13th, as the coast was not yet clear of submarines, he was ordered into Plymouth Sound, and at 5.45 a.m. on the 14th, when Bishop Rock light (Scilly Isles) was abeam, all ships, in accordance with the latest order, were steaming through a heavy sea and a northerly gale for Devonport; two hours later, on a signal from the flagship, the White Squadron hauled out of column to starboard, to form in line following the cruiser *Eclipse* at 15 knots. The first transports to arrive were the *Alaunia* and the *Montreal* which, having gone ahead under escort of the *Diana,* entered Plymouth Sound at 7.00 a.m. on September 13th., 1914.

The White Squadron ordered to proceed at full speed to Eddystone Lighthouse and thence to Penlee Point, took pilots aboard and proceeded into Plymouth Sound and thence to H.M. Dockyard, Devonport, England). The remaining ships, now with additional protection of cruisers and battleships, and surrounded by a fleet of torpedo-boat destroyers, followed, but had to lie in a choppy sea outside the breakwater waiting their turn to enter as pilots became available.

At 4.00 in the afternoon the *Charybdis* arrived at Devonport, but not until seven o'clock next evening was the Admiralty in a position to report—

### "All Canadian transports have arrived at Plymouth."

As ship after ship of the unexpected Canadian convoy moved up the Sound and dropped anchor in the Hamoaze, the townspeople of Plymouth and Devonport became aware that with the arrival of the first troops from overseas another historic event was taking place at their ancient harbour. Naval cadets dressed ship and cheered, church bells rang out, wondering crowds lined the waterfront and wharves, workmen building battleships dropped tools long enough to chalk "Bravo Canadians!" on the armour plate; women and children hurried aboard excursion steamers to make a tour about the transports. The Mayor of Plymouth, on behalf of the civil population, sent cordial greetings.

Lord Kitchener also welcomed the troops to the shores of the Mother Country.

Before going ashore each man, as provided in the charter- party, drew one day's dry ration from ship's stores, from which also were issued two feeds of oats per horse. Dismounted units, greeted enthusiastically by the citizens with cheers, cigarettes, kisses, drinks, and presentation copies of the New Testament, marched up the thronged streets direct from the docks to the railway station and entrained; the regimental transport and horses sometimes preceded, rarely accompanied, and sometimes followed. Mounted units usually spent a day in bivouac at the naval parade ground, so that the horses might recuperate from the fatigue of standing for three weeks on board ship; the days in harbour, with no breeze to ventilate between decks, had been hard on them, and more horses died in port than on the voyage—the casualties on shipboard totalled 86, about 1.13 per cent.

From Plymouth the trains carried the force across Devon and Dorset to stations in Wiltshire adjacent to Salisbury Plain—Lavington and Patney in the north, or Amesbury to the east.

The final march of eight or ten miles into camp was directed by a local policeman, the postman, or a boy scout. The horses, too weak for draught were walked under harness, and after the four days of gentle exercise
specified in Camp Orders, were fit to recover the vehicles
parked at railhead.

**Salisbury Plain,** where the force was destined to spend sixteen memorable weeks, is a broad hilly tract of three hundred square miles rising above the closely cultivated farmlands of southern Wiltshire and drained by the Avon and Wiley and their tributaries; a part of it, six miles by fifteen in extent, was War Department land which for a number of years had been used for field artillery and rifle ranges, and for summer camps and military manoeuvres.

While the convoy was crossing the Atlantic, preparation of camps on the Plain had been in progress, pitching tents, laying floors and building cookhouses.

On the 16th of October General Alderson established his headquarters at *Ye Olde Bustard,* a wayside inn in the middle of the Plain halfway between Salisbury and Devizes.

All villages in the vicinity of Salisbury Plain had already been placed out of bounds, except to men in possession of passes, and the order was enforced by military patrols.

## Let me digress about the ship Franconia.

The Franconia was the Headquarters ship with 2,300 troops on board. It always travelled in the center of this 21 mile long flotilla.

The **RMS Franconia** was an <u>ocean liner</u> operated by the <u>Cunard Line</u>, built in Britain and launched in July, 1910.

The Franconia was intended for the line's Boston service, with winter cruising service  between New York- and the Mediterranean. The Franconia could travel at a speed of 17 knots.

She had more bathrooms and showers on board than the Mauretania, which was the largest and fastest (23.69 knots (43.87 km/h; 27.26 mph.) of the Cunard line. The Franconia, unlike most cruise ships,  did not have staterooms on the upper deck, instead she had a library, gymnasium and a lounge and smoking room. Most definitely a comfortable ship for our Canadian nurses.

The RMS Franconia was used as a troop transport in 1915. However, on October 4th., 1916, while travelling to Salonika, she was torpedoed and sunk by the German U-boat UB-47 190 miles east of Malta.  Of her 314 crew members, 12 died.  The remainder were rescued by the hospital ship Dover Castle.


**On October 14th., 1914** Lieut.-General E.A.H. Anderson assumed command of all forces.

**On October 16th., 1914** Headquarters for the First Contingent was established at "The Bustard," **Salisbury Plain,** and on October 24th., Field Marshall Lord Roberts inspected the First Contingent.

**On October 21st.,** Princess Patricia's Canadian Light Infantry is assigned to the British 80th Brigade to become the **First Canadians troops in France.**

**On November 1st.,** four midshipmen of the R.C.N were lost in the Battle of Coronel.

**On this same date,** Great Britain and Turkey began hostilities

**On this same date,** the ships Good Hope and Mommouth were sunk by Admiral Von Spee's squadron.

**On November 2nd.,** A British force began an attack on Tanga (German East Africa) and the British force was repulsed three days later.

**On this same date,** a state of war started between Serbia and Turkey.

**On this same date,** Russia declared war on Turkey

**On this same date,** the British Admiralty declares the North Sea a military zone.

**On November 4th.,1914,** the King and Queen, accompanied by Lord Kitchener, inspect the First Contingent.

**On November 6th.,** Advance troops of the Indian Expeditionary Force landed in Mesopotamia.

**On November 7th., 1914** The Canadian Government ordered the mobilization of an additional 30,000 troops, including a Second Contingent.

**On November 8th** the **No 2 Canadian Hospital** arrives at **Boulogne** from Salisbury Plain. This was the first Canadian unit in France.


This letter explains the situation at the time quite well.

**From Red Cross Nurse. - Miss Harriet Graham-Dec., 1914 Canada No. 2 Stationary Hospital, France**


Dear---------------

I'm sorry not to have gotten a letter off to you before this, but we have been on the jump and have been awfully busy, and now I have all beds turned down and am waiting for the ambulances to come in with their loads.

It is great, and we love it. We have a dandy crowd of girls and a very nice crowd of officers, and our men are as willing as can be, though most of them are untrained: but when I see the poor souls scrubbing and doing all sorts of things they never did before, I can't but feel sorry for them. But I must start at the beginning of my story.

We have the most beautiful hospital you could imagine, and we are simply proud of ourselves, for the **FIRST Canadian Hospital** to be in France.

We just came here and commandeered a beautiful summer hotel, turned into it, and settled ourselves.

Then we took a house belonging to Count Constaudivitch, who married Miss Cutting of New York, and who is in Servia or someplace on war business, for the nurses to live in, and another for the officers. They are all right together, so it makes it quite nice, and a comfortable bed to turn into at night when we get off duty.

But our hospital is grand. There were big verandas on three sides, which have been enclosed in glass, and make fine wards.
I tell you, if you think house cleaning is hard work, and you know I do think it, I hope I don't have to clean another hotel; but we had some fun out of it too. Col. Shilling said he was going to name all the wards for the different provinces. So I said: "Well please put Nova Scotia in the dining room." The dining room , I must explain, is the biggest ward and right at the main entrance. "that's it 'J he said, "Sister Graham always wants Nova Scotia to have the biggest and best place right in front; that is the place for Ontario, as most of the corps come from there." One of the other girls said: "But British Columbia is the biggest province." "Well," I said, "We will all have to put the names in a hat and draw for it," and the fun of it is Nova Scotia has it – the prettiest ward, with seventy-five beds and the most important place.

We are all extremely pleased. I'm going to send to Dr. Neily and see if he can get a Nova Scotia flag for it. At present I am sitting in Quebec, as they are going to receive tonight.

Pearl Fraser is on night duty, but it is not so awful, or at least has not been so far, as the nights we receive we all stay in and help. You know, they always come in at night.

We have fifteen ambulances and they each carry four patients, and when they all make about three trips, it makes quite a number of patients.

I'm not allowed to tell you how many patients we have or how many we can take, but you can tell Kit we can take twice as many as St. Luke's, and, of course, may have to take more than that at any time. Oh! My, but it is great.

I just love it, even though it's ten o'clock now and I have been on the go all day, and they have not started to come in yet. I see where we don't get to bed tonight. By the time we get the poor souls into bed and half way clean and a dressing done, its morning before you know it, and the poor creatures, you would be sorry for them, they are so filthy, and many times just alive with vermin.

Pearl said tonight: "isn't it funny, in our hospital we despised men who were dirty, and here the worse they are, the better we like them." When they say, "keep away sister, I'm so dirty, but I have been in the trenches, and I haven't had a bath for so many weeks," I just feel like saying, "I honour your dirt-!"

I hear we are getting a consignment of Germans tonight. I wonder sometimes if it is a sin to feel so awful for our enemies. I don't know if there is much in the papers at home about, them and the awful things they do.

4 a.m. - The ambulances started to come just then, so I had to stop, and now must turn in, as 7 a.m. comes soon, and I will try to finish this tomorrow.

Dec. 4. – It is time again to go to bed, I suppose, but it seems to be the only time for letter writing, and I know how you all at home must look for a line, and then it seems so far to send a letter with nothing in it. When we get our hospital in better running order, we may have more time; though, of course, we are all dreading the spring and the diseases that must come in this war.

Our patients of last night are mostly happy today. I spend all the spare pennies I can find on cigarettes for them, poor boys, it seems to do more to quiet their nerves than anything else. I wish I could tell you some of their tales, but I'm afraid my letter would never go by the censor. One of my patients is just a lad of eighteen, and the nicest kind of a kid. He told me his two pals were shot and killed. I said: "Weren't you awfully afraid?" "Yes sister," he said, "I was awfully afraid at first; there was just thirty yards between the German trenches and ours; but I soon got over it.

You see sister, it's like this, there is no use trying to dodge them, if the bullet's for you, you'll get it." He then asked me if it would be long before he could go back. "Why", I said, "do you want to go back?" He just looked at me and said: "Does anybody want to go to Hell, sister?" and, poor kid, he will have to go back, because he is not very badly injured. Some of the tales they tell are awful, too terrible to write about. The "Jack Johnsons," as the Tommies call the German's big guns, are really devilish, and although we are as far from the firing as three-quarters of the way to Truro, still the guns can be heard quite distinctly at night. That will give you some idea what the noise must be close up, and is it any wonder that the poor boys' nerves are in most cases completely gone, - but I must not write of such things.

Miss McDonald was here to see us, and we were so glad to have her. She is so nice, and I get fonder of her all the time. If we are here, and if she can manage it, and a few more "ifs" she is coming to spend Christmas with us. I suppose it will be nearly Christmas before you get this, possibly after. Give my love and best wishes to all the friends.

I received some Halifax papers last night from Mr. Neilly, one of which gave a list of the Pictou County boys going in the next contingent. I was sorry not to see more familiar names from New Glasgow. I am afraid they don't realize what this war means. I tell you it's awful to think of when our boys come over, but I would be ashamed if Wendell was any place but right where he is now.

Well, I must stop and turn in.

HARRIET

**NOTES:** The First Canadian Hospital (CSH) referred to in the letter, was the first unit to set foot in France with the original staff qualifying for the "Mons Star" given to people serving in the war before Dec 31st., 1914.

This letter was written in 1914, to her parents, Harvey and Hannah Graham, both of whom are resting in Riverside Cemetery in New Glasgow.

**Harriet Graham,** (the writer of this letter) Daughter of Harvey Graham, 1848-1907  was born in 1883 in New Glasgow and died in 1932. * buried at Riverside Cemetery.

**Wendell Stewart Graham**, Harriet's brother born 1879, also served in the first war and died in 1945. * Buried at Riverside Cemetery.

**Marjorie  (Pearl) Fraser**  was the daughter of  D.C. and Bessie Fraser and a 1$^{st}$ cousin to Wendell and Harriet.  Marjorie was born in 1884 and died in 1918 when the Hospital Ship Llandovery Castle Hospital ship was torpedoed. Marjorie is remembered on a Monument with her brother Alistair and Laurie Fraser in Riverside Cemetery in New Glasgow, Laurier died  in France 3 months before his sister Marjorie.

His funeral in France was attended by his uncle Major Roderick Douglas Graham.

A stained glass window is in Marjorie's church in New Glasgow to her memory.

**Status and Control:**

The British War Office considered the Canadian Contingent a Division which seem a simple chain of command. However, the Canadian Minister of Militia complicated matters for the British.

He, **General Sir Sam Hughes**,  wore the Canadian uniform and there was no room to doubt that he was an officer of the Canadian Militia and a Minister representing the Government of Canada.

Sir Sam was invited to a meeting with Lord Kitchener. Sir Sam marched up to Kitchener's desk. When he arrived at the desk Kitchener spoke up quickly and in a very stern voice said:

"Hughes, I see you have brought over a number of men from Canada; they are of course without training and this would apply to their officers; I have decided to divide them up among the British regiments; they will be of very little use to us as they are." Sir Sam replied:

"Sir, do I understand you to say that you are going to break up these Canadian regiments that came over? Why, it will kill recruiting in Canada." Lord Kitchener answered "You have your orders, carry them out." Sir Sam replied: "I'll be damned if I will," turned on his heel and marched out.

He immediately cabled to Sir Robert Borden the disturbing news of this change in policy, and interviewed the British Prime Minister (Mr. Asquith) and the Chancellor of the Exchequer (Mr. Lloyd George). Within a few days the order was rescinded; it was decided that the Canadian units should not be broken up but should be kept together to operate and fight in Canadian formations in the field.

**Weather:**

At Salisbury Plain in the 123 days, from mid-October 1914 to mid-February 1915, rain fell on 89 days.

The average precipitation for that period, over the preceding thirty-two years was 11.98 inches; this was almost exactly doubled, and there was widespread flooding in the river valleys.

From 21st October, when the weather broke, and a quarter inch of rain fell, conditions in all camps grew worse. An inch fell in the next five days; it was cold and raw, with occasional frosts at night, and there were no facilities for drying clothing.

On 2nd November more than an inch of rain fell; in the high winds the light tents afforded little protection, and the number of blankets per man was increased from three to four. On the 11th of November a wind-storm blew down most of the marquees and all of the divisional headquarters tents but one.

Rain, fog, frost and mud, from which there was no respite, made life miserable for men and horses. On 4th December, a sudden gale once more flattened much of the canvas, scattered beyond recovery correspondence in office tents, and blew away the treasury notes of a pay parade. Next day there was rain, hail and frost.

It had been suggested to Lord Kitchener by Colonel Carson, as representative of the Minister of Militia, that the Contingent should be moved for training to Egypt.

Rumours of a possible move to Egypt reached the Canadians on Salisbury Plain and raised visions of dry blankets and cloudless skies, but nothing came of it.

H.M. FORCES OVERSEAS (IN UNIFORM).

COMBINED LEAVE AND RAILWAY TICKET.

Available for an authorised journey on the Railways in Great Britain and Ireland (including the Metropolitan and Metropolitan District Railways) and on the Steamers running to and from the Ports.

NOT available on the London Tube Railways.

No. B 309697    Third Class,

FOR ONE PERSON ONLY.

**Leave:**

From the first arrival in England leave not exceeding six days for all ranks up to twenty per cent of the force was allowed, with a free ticket to any place in the British Isles.

**The common name for this was a "Blighty Pass" permitting leave and transportation.  At the time, in England, the word "Blighty" meant almost anything.**

On 6th November the G.O.C., reduced the percentage "owing to the numerous reports he had had of considerable numbers of men being drunk and disorderly in public places of entertainment in London and other towns."

The restriction was removed in mid-December when half the Contingent was allowed six days leave for Christmas, and the other half a similar period at New Year. However, on 26th January all leave was cancelled and all on leave were recalled.

Whenever the Canadian troops could emerge from the Plain they were met with kindness and consideration. The local villagers, the citizens of Salisbury, and indeed the whole population of the British Isles, extended the warmest hospitality to the men from overseas.

**Training:**

For training, the whole area of the Salisbury Plain at the disposal of the Contingent was divided into four parts on 22nd of October:

> ➤ Bustard Camp area in the southeast for all troops;
> ➤ West Down South and West Down North camps in the southwest, for all except Divisional Mounted Troops and artillery units;
> ➤ Pond Farm Camp, to the west, for all troops except cavalry;
> ➤ Also a larger area to the northeast for cavalry and artillery.

These four camp areas were each under an O.C.—the Camp Commandant—who made further subdivision, and who had direction of route marches of progressive length to be carried out by all units three times a week.

The degree of preparedness of the troops having been gauged, a syllabus of training for the ensuing week was issued on 7th November; this was followed a week later by another laid out to occupy thirteen weeks. The whole plan was carried out under direction of the Southern Command, which issued notes on training; prominence was given to exercises stressed in War Office comments on the syllabus, and to special features brought out in "Notes from the Front" prepared at G.H.Q. in France.

Most of the instruction was given by officers of the Contingent, but two officers and five n.c.o. instructors were loaned by the War Office for special duty. They were experts in Bayonet fighting.

Special areas were set apart for practice in trench digging, and it was stringently enforced that the party which had dug the trench should, before leaving, refill the trench and replace the turf.

A weekly syllabus for each infantry battalion was drawn up by the O.C. and submitted for approval. In these there was little variation: physical training, one hour daily throughout the period; musketry instruction, twenty-seven hours for the first three weeks; drill, fifteen hours per week, and night work, outposts, route marching and entrenching from two to four hours per week.

In general, five weeks were allotted to company training, two to battalion training and two hours to brigade training.

## In the final outcome, Canadian Forces were trained to the highest degree.

**On November 9th., 1914,** the German Cruiser Emden was destroyed by H.M.A.S. Sydney at Cocos Island (Australia).

On the same date, The British Prime Minister declares: "We shall never sheathe the sword, which we have not lightly drawn, until Belgium recovers in full measure all and more than all that she has sacrificed, until France is adequately secured against the menace of aggression, until the rights of the smaller nationalities of Europe are placed upon an unassailable foundation, and until the military domination of Prussia is wholly and finally destroyed."

**On this same date,** a detachment, 350 strong, attended the Lord Mayor's Show in London and marched in the procession, led by Colonel V. A. S. Williams.

**On November 10th.,** Przemysl (Southeastern Poland) is again isolated by Russian forces and the Second siege begins and didn't end until March 22nd., 1915.

**On November 15th.,** the Battle of Cracow (Galicia) began and ended on December 2nd. 1914.

**On November 16th.,** the second German offensive took place against Warsaw. It was the Battle of Lodz, which ended on Dec. 15th.

**On November 19th.,** A small detachment from Camp Salisbury, represented the Canadian forces at the burial of their Colonel-in-Chief, Field-Marshal Earl Roberts, V.C., at St. Paul's Cathedral on 19th November: he had died at the age of 82 while on an inspection tour of the Indian troops in France. Over 400 officers and men attended the simultaneous memorial service held in Salisbury Cathedral, while the Royal Canadian Horse Artillery fired a salute of nineteen guns.

On **November 22ⁿᵈ.,** 1914, Basra (Mesopotamia) was occupied by British forces.

On **November 26ᵗʰ.,** the H.M.S. Bulwark was destroyed by an internal explosion in Sheerness Harbour

On **November 30ᵗʰ.,1914,** The Battle of Lowicz-Sannika (Russian Poland) began and ended on December 17ᵗʰ.,

**On this same date,** Belgrade was evacuated by Serbian forces (Occupied by Austrians on December 2ⁿᵈ., 1914.

On **December 1ˢᵗ.,1914,** The Battle of Limanova-Lapanow (Galicia) began and ended on December 17ᵗʰ.

On **December 3ʳᵈ.,** The Battle of Kolubare (Serbia) began and ended on December 6ᵗʰ., 1914.

On **December 5ᵗʰ.,** the Serbian Government declares that the Serbian Government will never make peace without allied consent.

**December 8ᵗʰ., 1914,** The Battle of the Falklands took place and Admiral Von Spee's squadron was destroyed. The Sharnhorst, Gneisenau, Leipzig and Nurn-berg were sunk and the Dresden escaped.

On **December 13ᵗʰ., 1914,** the Turkish battleship Messudiyeh was sunk by the British submarine in the Dardanelles (the only waterway between the Black Sea in the east and the Mediterranean Sea in the west.)

On **December 14ᵗʰ.,** Fighting in Flanders begins and continued until December 20ᵗʰ., 1914.

On **December 16ᵗʰ., 1914** The British coastal towns of Scarborough and Hartlepool were bombarded by the German battle cruiser squadron. Two German battleships, Derfflinger and Von der Tann, bombarded the Yorkshire seaside town of Scarborough for about half an hour.

During that short period over 500 shells rained down on the castle and town, killing 17 inhabitants and injuring many more.

The castle was the prime target although it was now only used for storage. The Houses across the town had walls blown out, roofs ripped off and windows smashed by shellfire. There was widespread panic as people quite thought the bombardment was the start of a German invasion.

**On December 17th., 1914** The Turkish offensive in Caucasus (Russia) began.

**On December 18th., 1914,** Britain claimed to be a protectorate of Egypt.

**On December 20th.,** The Newfoundland Regiment leaves the Contingent for Fort George, Scotland.

**On this same date,** The first Battle of Champagne began and continued until March 17th., 1915.

**On this same date,** The British were defending Givenchy.

**On December 21st., 1914** the P.P.C.L.I. (Princess Patricia's Canadian Light Infantry) lands at Le Havre – The first Canadian Combatant unit in France.

Christmas Truce

britannica.com

**On this same date,** was the first German Air Raid on Britain.

**On December 25th., 1914,** shortly after midnight on Christmas morning, the German troops engaged in World War 1, ceased all warlike actions. The guns stopped, as did the war for this period of time and all the soldiers on all sides began to sing Christmas Carols. Brass bands were heard from the Germans.

At dawn's first light, many of the German soldiers cautiously left their trenches and came across no-man's-land, calling out **"Merry Christmas"** in their enemies' native tongues. The Allied soldiers feared it was a trick, but seeing the Germans unarmed, they came out of their trenches and shook hands with the enemy soldiers.

The men exchanged presents of cigarettes and plum puddings and sang carols and songs. There was even a documented case of soldiers from opposing sides playing a good-natured game of soccer.

Some soldiers, on both sides, used this ceasefire time for the retrieval of the bodies of fellow soldiers who had fallen within the no-man's land between the lines.

The so-called Christmas Truce of 1914 came only five months after the outbreak of war in Europe and was one of the last examples of chivalry between enemies in warfare.

**On December 26th., 1914**, 11,133 of the First Contingent were still under canvas at Salisbury Plain; the remaining 19,204 were housed in huts and billets.

**On December 28th., 1914** The organized rebellion in South Africa ceased. This was known as the **Maritz rebellion**, also known as the **Boer revolt** or **Five Shilling rebellion.** This was an armed insurrection which occurred in **South Africa** in 1914 at the start of World War I, led by **Boers** who supported the reestablishment of the **South African** Republic in the Transvaal.

**On December 29th., 1914,** the Battle of Sarikamish (Russia's Kars Province), began and continued until January 2nd., 1915.

**On January 1st., 1915,** the H.M.S. Formidable was sunk by a German submarine in the English Channel.

**On January 4th.,1915,** It was proclaimed to be a day of Humble Prayer and Intercession.

**On January 8th., 1915**, the Battle of Soissons (a French town on the bank of the Aisne River) began and concluded on January 14th.

**On January 11th., 1915,** The last rebels in the Transvaal were captured (**Transvaal** was a province of South Africa from 1910 until 1994).

**On January 13th., 1915,** The British War Council resolved that the Admiralty should prepare for a naval expedition in February  against the Dardanelles. (As the only waterway between the Black Sea in the east and the Mediterranean Sea in the west the area was contested from the beginning of the war.)

**On January 14th., 1915,** Swakopmund (German South Africa) was occupied.

**On January 18th., 1915,** Infantry battalions converted from 8 companies to 4 double companies. A Canadian Training Depot was established at Tidworth in Wiltshire, England.

**January 19th., 1915,** The first German Zeppelin raid occurred on the British mainland.

**On January 20th., 1915.** Selection made of units and personnel of the First Canadian Contingent to form let (4th) Canadian Division.

**On January 24ᵗʰ., 1915,** The German cruiser Blucher was sunk by the Dogger Bank (a large sandbank in a shallow area of the North Sea about 100 kilometres (62 mi) off the east coast of England).

**On January 25ᵗʰ., 1915** the first action of Givenchy, a large farming village in France north of Arras, took place. It was better known as Givenchy-en-Gohelle.
It was on the front line between German and Allied forces during the battles of Arras and was severely damaged, particularly during the Battle of Vimy Ridge in 1917.

Givenchy-en-Gohelle was taken by the 2nd Canadian Division on 13 April 1917. Over 150 war casualties (1914-1918) are commemorated at the Canadian cemetery here and 109 from the Battle of Vimy Ridge are buried here.

**January 28ᵗʰ., 1915,** The British Government decides to make naval attacks on the Dardanelles. ( The Dardanelles were a 60 mile-long narrow strip of heavily fortified water dividing Europe from Asia.)

**On January 30ᵗʰ., 1915,** The Canadian Cavalry Brigade formed to consist of R.C.D., L.S.H., 2nd King Edward's Horse and R.C.H.A. Brig. General J. E. B. Seely to command.

**On January 31ˢᵗ., 1915,** Marked the first use of Poison Gas in WW 1 by Germany at Bolimow in Poland on the Eastern Front.

**On February 3ʳᵈ., 1915,** The Turkish attach on the Suez canal began and ended the following day.

**On February 4ᵗʰ., 1915,** The winter battle in Masuria (East Prussia) began and ended on the 22ⁿᵈ.

**On February 4ᵗʰ., 1915,** His Majesty, the King, accompanied by Lord Kitchener Inspected the 1ˢᵗ. Canadian Division on Salisbury Plain

**On this same date,** Parliament opened and was Prorogued until April 15ᵗʰ., 1915.

**On February 7th., 1915,** The movement of the 1st. Canadian Division by rail to Avonmouth, England for embarkation to France began. (Avonmouth, at the time had one of the largest docks in the UK.).

**On February 12th., 1915,** H.Q., and the 1st Canadian Division lands at St. Nazaire in western France.

**On this same date,** 1 British, 2 Anzac and 2 Indian Infantry Divisions were now in Egypt.   1 Indian Infantry Division was in Mesopotamia.

**On February 15th., 1915,** Disembarkation   at St. Nazaire was complete.

**On February 16th., 1915,** the British Government decided to send a division to the Dardanelles. They arrived on the 29th. of February.

**On February 18th., 1915,** the German submarine blockade of Great Britain began.

**On February 19th., 1915** the Allied attack on the Dardanelles Forts Began. This narrows was an extremely important area.

The fortresses had been built to cover a minefield, which in August 1914 was a line of mines across the strait from Kephez Point to the European shore.

* This is one of the more interesting stories to research.

You will also note submarine nets at each end of the waterway. Fort Dardanos was the main area which had two new 6-inch naval guns and the rest contained ten small Quick-firing guns with shields. At the Narrows, the Inner Defences had the heaviest guns and some mobile light howitzers and field guns. Five forts had been built on the European side and six on the Asian side with 72 heavy and medium guns.

This 60 mile long, narrow strip of water separated Europe from Asia and had great strategic significance. The Dardanelles was under and international treaty.

The closing of the Dardanelles with submarine nets and other means, helped to bring the Ottoman empire into the war as German allies in 1914. Great Britain and France attempted to attack Constantinople (Istanbul) by way of the Dardanelles.

Winston Churchill felt that if they could succeed at this it would help Russia and secure the Suez Canal and their oil interests. However as you read on the the attack on Feburary 19th., 1914 was only the start of this assault. On January, 1916 the allies, after heavy losses, the attack was abandoned and troops evacuated.

**On February 20th., 1915,** Orders issued for deployment at the Dardanelles of the Australian and New Zealand troops in Egypt.

**On February 22nd. 1915,** First Battle of Przasnysz begins.

**On February 22nd., 1915,** Australian and New Zealand troops were first employed in Egypt.

**On this same date,** the first unit of the Canadian Railway troops was authorized.

**On February 24th., 1915,** The first British Territorial Division (the North Midland) leaves England for France.

**On February 26th., 1915,** Liquid fire first used by Germans on the Western front.

**On February 28th., 1915,** The British casualties to date on Western front, killed, died, wounded and prisoners, total 111,391.

**On March 1st., 1915.,** Britain and France signed a declaration to prevent trade by or with Germany.

**On March 3rd., 1915,** 1st Canadian Division under IV Corps, First Army, takes over Fleurbaix sec-tor. H.Q. at Sailly-sur-la-Lys.

**On March 5th., 1915,** The bombardment of Smyma ( Greek city located at a strategic point on the Aegean coast of Anatolia) by the British began and ended on March 9th.,

**On March 10th., 1915,** The Battle of Neuve Chapelle, let Canadian Division co-operates on the flank by a fire attach during the first assault. The battle ended on the 13th. Of March.

**On March 11th., 1915,** The Canadian Training Division was established at Shorncliffe, (England) commanded by Brig-General J.C. MacDougall.

**On March 14th., 2015,** The Cruiser Dresden, the last German cruiser was sunk off Juan Fernandez (West coast of Chile) by German warships.

**On March 26th., 1915,** No. 6 Company R.C.G.A. sailed from Halifax to St. Lucia, B.W.I.
**On March 27th., 1915,** the 1st. Canadian Division was withdrawn into Reserve. H.Q, at Estaires in Northern France.

**On April 1st., 1915,** The 1st Canadian Division was transferred to the Second Army and proceeded to march to the area between Cassel and Poperinghe. H.Q. at Oxecaere (a small village in the north of France).

**On April 8th., 1915,** the German merchant cruiser Prinz Eitel Fredrick, a smaller liner of 8,797 tons, having a surface speed of 15 knots operated from the 5th. of August 1914 to the 8th. of April 1915.

In all she accounted for 11 ships of 33,424 tons, but this raider was running short of supplies, and her increasing number of prisoners exacerbated this problem of feeding both the crew and her captives.

Captain Thierichens decided to enter the American port of Newport News on the eastern coast of America on the 11th. of March 1915, and they were interned. The ship was seized and served as a troopship renamed *De Kalb*.

The US American Lines Inc. bought the ship in 1921, another name was used, and as *Mount Clay*, she served only for 3 years, to be broken up in 1935.

**On this same date,** the massacre of Armenians by the Turkish Government began.

**On April 12<sup>th</sup>., 1915,** The Battle of Shaiba (Mesopotamia) began and concluded on the 14<sup>th</sup>.

**On this same date,** The first advance on Younde (Cameroon) began and ended on the 28<sup>th</sup> of June.

**On April 14<sup>th</sup>., 1915,** the Germans accused the French of using poison gas near Verdun.

**On this same date,** the British Secretary for the Colonies states that the Dominion will be consulted as to peace terms.

**On this same date,** The Japanese Government informed the British Government of the request by Germany for a separate peace.

**On April 17<sup>th</sup>., 1915,** the 1<sup>st</sup>. Canadian Division took over the line in the northern face of Ypres salient. H.Q. near Brielin.

**On this same date,** fighting at Hill 60 (south of Ypres) began.

Hill 60 had been captured by the German 30th Division on November 11<sup>th</sup>., 1914, during the First Battle of Ypres (19 October – November 22<sup>nd</sup>., 1914). Initial

French preparations to raid the hill were continued by the British 28th Division, which took over the line in February 1915 and then by the 5th Division.

The plan was expanded into an ambitious attempt to capture the hill, despite advice that Hill 60 could not be held unless the nearby **Caterpillar Ridge** was also occupied. It was found that Hill 60 was the only place in the area not waterlogged and a French 3 ft. × 2 ft mine gallery was extended.

Miners from Northumberland and Wales were recruited for the digging and the British attack began again on 17 April 1915. The hill was captured quickly with only seven casualties but then it was found that the salient (bulge) which had been created, made occupation of the hill very costly. Both sides mistakenly accused the other of using

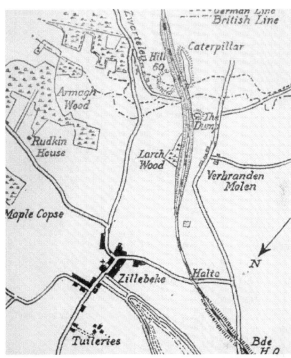

poison gas in the April fighting; German attacks on the hill in early May included the use of gas shells and the Germans recovered the ground at the second attempt on 5 May. It remained in German hands until the Battle of Messines in 1917,

**On April 20th., 1915,** British Divisions were now on the Western Front which included: 5 Cavalry divisions, including two Indian units, 18 Infantry Units including one Canadian unit and two Indian units, together holding 36 miles of line.

**On April 22nd., 1915,** The Battle of Ypres (1915) began and ended on May 25th with the gas attack.

**1** Hill 60
**2** Mont Sorrel
**3** Tor Top
**4** Maple Copse
**5** Sanctuary Wood

Perhaps this map will put things in better perspective.

**On April 22 & 23rd., 1915,** The battle of Gravenstafel Ridge (Ypres) with the first Gas attack.

**On April 24 – 30th., 1915,** The Battle of St. Julien Started and continued to May 4th. This was the first instance of the Germans using gas.

**On April 25th., 1915,** Allied Forces landed at Dardanelles.

**On April 26th., 1915,** The last German raider overseas, Kronprinz Wilhelm, interned at Newport News, USA,

**On this same date,** a secret agreement (The Treaty of London) was signed in London between Italian Government and the Entente for Italian co-operation in the war and declaration by which Italy adheres to the Pact of London. Italy renounced its membership in the Triple Alliance, on May 4th., 1915, and joined Britain and its allies in the war against Austria-Hungary.

After the war, Italy lost the territory of the Dalmatian coast, which became a part of Yugoslavia under Marshall Tito.

**On April 28th., 1915,** The first battle of Krithia (Dardanelles)

**On May 1st., 1915,** The Austro-German spring offensive began in Galicia. The Battle of Gorlice-Tarnow began and ended on the 5th.

**On May 4th., 1915,** The 1st. Canadian Division withdrew to G.H.Q. Reserve between Merris, Bailleul and Nieppe. H.Q. Nieppe.

**On May 6th., 1915,** The second Battle of Krithia (Gallipoli peninsula) began and ended on the 8th.

**On May 7th., 1915,** the SS Lusitonia, a Cunard ocean liner, was sunk by the German submarine, U. 20, off Queenstown. Of the 1900 passengers, over 1,100 perished, including more than 120 Americans. This was one incident that helped encourage the Americans to enter the war.

**On May 8th., 1915,** Dismounted detachment Cdn. Cav. Bde., 1,500 strong, joins lot Canadian Division.

**On this same date,** The Battle of Frezenberg Ridge (Ypres) begins (ends 13th May).

**On May 9th., 1915,** The Allied spring offensive began with the Battle of Aubers Ridge and the second Battle of Artois which ended on June 18th.

**On May 10th., 1915,** The H.M.S. Goliath sunk by Turkish destroyer in the Dardanelles.

**On May11<sup>th</sup>., 1915**, the French captured the fort and chapel of Notre Dame de Lorette.

**On May 12<sup>th</sup>., 1915,** the French captured Carency (north of France).

**On May 13<sup>th</sup>.,1915,** Windhoek (German S.W. Africa), occupied.

**On May 15<sup>th</sup>., 1915,** the First Canadian Division marched to an area N.W. of Bethune, and were at the disposal of the First Army.

**On this same date,** the 4<sup>th</sup>. Canadian Infantry Brigade H.Q left Davenport proceeding to the Canadian Forces Camp at West Sandling, near Saltwood, Kent.

**On this same date,** the Battle of Festubert began and continued until the 25<sup>th</sup>. The Battle of Festubert was the continuation of the Battle of Aubers Ridge (9 May) and part of the larger French Second Battle of Artois. The resumption of the British offensive was intended to assist the French Tenth Army offensive against Vimy Ridge near Arras, by attracting German divisions to the British front, rather than reinforcing the defenders opposite the French. This would be the first British army night attack of the war.

The battle was preceded by a 60-hour bombardment by 433 artillery pieces that fired about 100,000 shells. This bombardment failed to significantly damage the front line defenses of the German 6th Army but the initial advance made some progress in good weather conditions. The attack was renewed on 16 May and by 19 May the 2nd Division and 7th Division had to be withdrawn due to heavy losses. On 18 May, the 1st Canadian Division, assisted by the 51st (Highland) Division, attacked but made little progress in the face of German artillery fire.

The British forces dug in at the new front line in heavy rain. The Germans brought up reinforcements and reinforced their defenses.
From 20–25 May the attack was resumed and Festubert was captured. The offensive had resulted in a 3-kilometre (1.9 mi) advance concluding on May 25<sup>th</sup>.

**On May 19th., 1915,** the 1st. Canadian Division Takes over Festubert sector, as part of Alderson's force. H.Q. Locon.

**On this same date,** Defence of Anzac, Dardanelles continued.

**On May 21st., 1915,** Russian Expeditionary Force to West Persia lands at Enzeli.

**On May 22nd., 1915,** 1st Canadian Division transferred in line to I Corps.

**On May 23rd., 1915,** 1st Canadian Division Headquarters at Halts, 5,000 x W. of Festubert.

**On this same date,** the Italian Government mobilized their troops and declared war against Austria.

**On May 24th., 1915,** Battle of Bellewaarde Ridge. (Ypres) and ended on the 25th.

**On this same date,** Germany severs diplomatic relations with Italy.

**On May 25th., 1915,** 2nd Canadian Division formed in England. Major-General Sam Steele takes command.

**On this same date,** Italian forces cross Austrian frontier (midnight 24th/25th)

**On this same date,** The H.M.S. Triumph was sunk by a submarine off the Dardanelles.

**On May 27th., 1915,** The British squadron joins Italian fleet in the Adriatic.

**On this same date,** The H.M.S. Majestic sunk by submarine off the Dardanelles.

**On May 28th., 1915,** The 8th Canadian Infantry Brigade disembarks Devonport and proceeds to Shorncliffe.

**On May 31st., 1915,** 1st Canadian Division was transferred in line to IV Corps.

**On this same date,** French take Souchez Refinery.

**On this same date,** The Second Action of Qurna (Mesopotamia): advance up the Tigris began and ended October 5th.

**On June 1st., 1915,** The 1st Canadian Division sideslips to occupy Givenchy sector. H.Q., Vendin-lezBethune

**On June 2nd., 1915,** A Commission of Inquiry into war purchases appointed.

**On this same date,** The Germans captured Hooge Chateau.

**On June 3rd., 1915,** Przemysl retaken by Austro-German forces. Amara (Mesopotamia) captured.

**On this same date,** First meeting of Allied Conference on economic war (in Paris).

**On June 4th., 1915,** Third Battle of Krithia. (Dardanelles)

**On June 5th., 1915,** First Conference of British and French Ministers to co-ordinate war policy and strategy, held at Calais.

**On June 6th., 1915,** The French action near Quennevières begins and ended on the 18th.

**On June 7th., 1915,** The French action near Hebuterne begins.

**On this same date,** A German Zeppelin was destroyed in mid-air near Ghent: the first one successfully attacked by aeroplane.

**On this same date,** The First meeting of the Dardanelles Committee of the Cabinet took place.

**On June 8th., 1915,** The French held all Neuville St. Vaast and make progress in "the Labyrinth."

**On June 10th., 1915,** Garua (Cameroons) capitulates.

**On June 13th., 1915,** The 1st Canadian Division re-armed with Short Magazine Lee-Enfield. Ross rifle discarded.

**On June 15th., 1915,** The Army Council suggests that the two Canadian divisions be formed into an Army Corps.

**On this same date,** The Second Action of Givenchy began and ended on the 18th.

**On June 16th., 1915,** The First attack on Bellewaarde began.

**On June 17th., 1915,** The third Battle of Lemberg Began and finished on the 22nd.

**On June 19th., 1915,** The advance on Otavifontein (German S.W. Africa) begins. (Captured by South African forces 1st July).

**On June 20th., 1915,** German attacks in the Argonne began and ended on 24th July.

**On June 21st., 1915,** The 1st C.M.M.G. Brigade from England attached to lot Canadian Division.

**On June 22nd., 1915,** Lemberg was retaken by Austrian forces.

**On June 23rd., 1915,** The French Armies organized into three groups.

**On June 24th., 1915,** The 1st Cdn. Div. was withdrawn into the First Army Reserve.

**On this same date,** The Army Council suggests the raising of a third division.

**On June 27th., 1915,** The British advance up the Euphrates (The longest river in southwest Asia) begins.

**On June 28th., 1915,** The 1st Cdn. Div. under III Corps, Second Army, takes over frontage opposite Messines. H.Q., Nieppe.

**On this same date,** The Action of Gully Ravine (Dardanelles).

**On June 29th., 1915,** The First battle of the Isonzo (the Isonzo River is on the eastern sector of the Italian Front) begins and ended on July 7th.

**On June 30th., 1915,** A Hospital Commission was appointed for the care of the sick and wounded in Canada.

**On this same date,** the Prime Minister of Canada sails for England for personal conference with British Government.

**On July 1st., 1915,** The Canadian Minister of Militia and Defence leaves Ottawa for overseas.

**On July 2nd., 1915,** The Ministry of Munitions formed in Great Britain.

**On July 7th., 1915,** First inter-allied military conference at Chantilly.
**On July 8th., 1915,** Further mobilization of overseas forces was authorized: not to exceed 150,000, including those already raised and garrisons and guards in Canada.

**On July 9th., 1915,** German S.W. Africa capitulates to General Louis Botha. * General Louis Botha fought in the Boer war, Was Prime Minister of the Union of South Africa when Britain declared war in 1914, and led his country once again, this time against Germany.

**On July 11th., 1915,** The German light cruiser Konigsberg destroyed in Rufiji River by British monitors.

**On July 13<sup>th</sup>., 1915,** The Great Austro-German offensive on Eastern front begins.

**On July 14<sup>th</sup>., 1915,** A Dominion Premier (Sir Robert Borden, Canada) for the first time attends meeting of the British Cabinet.

**On July 15<sup>th</sup>., 1915,** The 1st Cdn. Div. transferred in line to II Corps.

**On July 16<sup>th</sup>.,1915,** The H.M.C.S. Niobe and Rainbow to be maintained at the expense of the Canadian Government.

**On July 17<sup>th</sup>., 1915,** The 2nd Cdn. Div. reviewed at Beachborough Park, Kent, by the Prime Minister of Canada and the Minister of Militia and Defence.

**On July 18<sup>th</sup>., 1915, The** Second Battle of the Isonzo began and ended 10th Aug.

**On July 19<sup>th</sup>., 1915,** The First Action of Hooge (Belgium) began.

**On July 20-27<sup>th</sup>., 1915,** Canadian Prime Minister Sir Robert Borden was visiting Canadian troops in France.

**On July 21<sup>st</sup> ., 1915,** Ivangorod (Russian Poland) invested.

**On July 25<sup>th</sup>., 1915,** The British Government guarantees cession of Mitylene to Greece.

**On July 30<sup>th</sup>., 1915,** Second Action of Hooge: Germans attack with liquid fire. Basically it was a flamethrower. The German soldier had a tank of liquid gas strapped on himself and he moved forward as a flamethrower. This was new to the allied troops. It was a walking gas pump sending flame for close to 100 feet. It was not the safest weapon for the soldier to be using.

**On this same date,** The Pope sends appeal for peace to belligerent Governments.

**On August 4th., 1915,** A review of 2nd Canadian Division at Shorncliffe by the Secretary of State for the Colonies and the Minister of Militia and Defence took place.

**On this same date,** Warsaw, Poland was occupied by German forces

**On August 5-14th.,** 1915, The Minister of Militia and Defense visited the troops in France.

**On August 6th., 1915,** The landing at Suvla (Dardanelles) begins and continued until the 15th.

**On this same date,** The Battle of Sari Bair (Dardanelles) begins and ended on the 10th.

**On August 8th., 1915,** The Turkish battleship Barbarousse-Haireddine sunk by British submarine.

**On August 9th., 1915,** The Third Action of Hooge took place. * Another chapter talks about the mining required in this area and others.

**About this same date,** British soldiers were issued with tin hats to replace the cloth ones they had used for the past year.

**On August 12th., 1915,** Br.-Gen. R. E. W. Turner, V.C., recalled from 3rd Cdn. Inf. Bde. to take over command of the 2nd Cdn. Div. in England.

**On this same date,** First ship sunk by torpedo from British seaplane.

**On August 13th., 1915,** The H.M.T. Royal Edward sunk in Aegean by German submarine. Loss of 865 officers and men, and 132 crew.

**On August 14th., 1915,** The No. 5 Cdn. Stationary Hospital arrives Cairo, Egypt.

**On August 16th., 1915,** The No. 1 Cdn. Stationary Hospital arrives Lemnos (Greek island in the northern part of the Aegean Sea.)

**On August 17th., 1915,** The No, 3 Cdn. Stationary Hospital arrives Lemnos.

**On this same date,** Kowno (Lithuania) stormed by German forces.

**On August 21st., 1915,** The Battle of Scimitar Hill (Dardanelles).

**On this same date,** Italy declares war on Turkey.

**On August 25th, 1915,** Brest-Litovsk (Russian Poland) captured by the Germans

**On August 30th., 1915,** An offer was made to Serbia that the Allies would guarantee the eventual freedom and self-determination of Bosnia, Herzegovina, South Dalmatia, Slavonia and Croatia.

**On August 31st., 1915,** Total Canadian troops in France 21,581; in England 46,195; in Canada 61,777.

**On September 2nd ., 1915,** H.M. The King, accompanied by Lord Kitchener, inspects 2nd Cdn. Div. at Beachborough Park, Shorncliffe.

**On September 3rd., 1915,** The Prime Minister and Minister of Militia and Defence arrive Ottawa from England.

**On this same date,** Grodno (Russia) captured by the Germans.

**On September 7th., 1915,** The Russian counter-attack in Galicia: Battle of Tarnopol begins and ended on the 16th.

**On September 9th., 1915,** The R.C.H.A. Bde. joins Canadian Cavalry Brigade under 1st Cdn. Div.

**On September 13<sup>th</sup>., 1915,** The Cdn. Corps was formed, consisting of 1st and 2nd Cdn. Divisions and Corps Troops, including Cdn. Cav. Bde. Corps H.Q. at Bailleul. Lieut-General E. A. H. Alderson, Corps Commander, Major General A. W. Currie commanding 1st Cdn. Div.

**On September 14-17<sup>th</sup>., 1915,** The movement of 2nd Cdn. Div. to France (Folkestone-Boulogne) began.

**On September 15<sup>th</sup>., 1915,** The H.Q., 2nd Cdn. Div. disembarks at Boulogne and moves to Caestre (France).

**On this same date,** Lord Kitchener announces 11 New Army Divisions sent to France.

**On September 17<sup>th</sup> – 27<sup>th</sup>., 1915,** The 3rd Bde., C.F.A., detached to 8th (British) Div. for action of Bois Grenier.

**On September 18<sup>th</sup>., 1915,** Vilna (Russia) was taken by German forces.

**On September 21<sup>st</sup>., 1915,** The Greek Premier asks for guarantee of 150,000 British and French troops as condition of Greek intervention.

**On September 22<sup>nd</sup>., 1915,** The Second advance on Yaunde (Cameroons) begins, ending on 31st Dec.

**On this same date,** The Dede Agatch Agreement concluded between Turkey and Bulgaria rectifying Turkey's frontier in favour of Bulgaria.

**On this same date,** The Bulgarian Government order general mobilization for 25th.

**On September 23<sup>rd</sup>., 1915,** The 2nd Cdn. Div. takes over sector in front of Kemmel.

**On September 24<sup>th</sup>., 1915,** The French and British Governments agree to Greek request of guarantees of the 21st.

**On September 25<sup>th</sup> ., 1915,** The Allied Autumn offensive begins:— Battle of Loos begins ending on Oct. 8<sup>th</sup>. Actions of Piètre and Bois Grenier and second attack on Bellewaarde.

**On this same date,** The Third Battle of Artois begins (ends 15th Oct.). Second Battle of Champagne begins (ends 6th Nov.).

**On this same date,** The British Divisions is now on the Western front: 5 Cavalry (including two Indian) and 36 Infantry (including two Canadian and two Indian), holding 70 miles of line.

**On this same date,** 1 British Mounted Division (dismounted)

**On this same date,** 8 British, 1 R.N. and 3 Anzac Infantry Divisions are now at the Dardanelles.

**On this same date,** 2 Indian Infantry Divisions now in Egypt.

**On this same date,** 2 Indian Infantry Divisions now in Mesopotamia.

**On this same date,** 3 British and 6 Indian Infantry Divisions are now garrisoning India.

**On September 27<sup>th</sup>., 1915,** King Constantine consents to proposed Entente expedition to Salonika

**On September 28<sup>th</sup> ., 1915,** The French attack reaches La Folie. Wood and Hill 145, are the highest point of Vimy Ridge; line subsequently withdrawn.

**On this same date,** Battle of Kut (Mesopotamia) began.

**On this same date,** Greek Government formally refuse guarantee of the 24th.

On September 30<sup>th</sup> ., 1915, British casualties to date on Western front: killed, died, wounded and prisoners, total 331,262, of which 11,779 Canadian.

On this same date, Lord Derby assumes control of British recruiting.

## The preceding is a chronology of World War 1 from July 23<sup>rd</sup>., 1914 to September 31th., 1915.

# CHAPTER 7

# CANADIAN BATTLES

At this point I will document the many Battles and actions in which Canadian Troops participated in on **ONLY** the Western Front.

### March 10<sup>th</sup>., - 13<sup>th</sup>.,1915,  The Battle of Neuve Chapelle:

This took place in the Artois region of France. The attack was the first planned offensive by the British Army and intended to cause a rupture in the German lines. British pilots dropped small bombs specifically to delay the German counterattack. This was one of the early uses of air support. 40,000 British, Canadian and Indian troops fought in this offensive. More than 11,000 Allied forces had been killed, including **100 Canadians killed and nearly 300 casualties**.

### March 14-15<sup>th</sup>., 1915, The Action at St. Eloi:

The Germans had an extensive system of tunnels under the land which were mined against the British trenches. The British suffered 500 casualties.

When the Germans captured Saint Eloi, they  penetrated British front-line trenches seizing important crossroads gaining vital high ground to dominate the surrounding area.

If 4th Battalion failed to retake the village, the entire British defense line in the Salient's southern shoulder would be at risk of collapse.

Shortly after 4 a.m. on March 15, 4th Battalion advanced along the Voormezeele-Saint Eloi road under cover of darkness. A half-hour later, D company moved south striking the enemy trench line, catching the Germans while they were still disorganized from their earlier attack, D Company quickly recaptured the position.

The battalion suffered over 100 casualties in the partially successful attack: 34 killed in action (including six officers), 63 wounded and six missing.

**\* More on St. Eloi further on.**

### April 22-23rd., 1915, Gravenstafel Ridge - First Gas Used.

After blowing the gas cloud across the sector held by two French divisions in the northern part of the Ypres Salient, the German attack on April 22nd., made significant advances into territory held by the Allies.

Most of the French and Algerian troops not asphyxiated by the poisonous gas left the front line in confusion. The German infantry, following on behind the gas cloud and at 5.15pm, the Germans successfully broke through the Allied front line.

**Pilckem Ridge**
**Courtesy of Wikipedia**

Within half an hour of the attack, the German Reserve Division in the centre of the attacking front had covered 3 to 4 kilometres of French-held ground and had reached its first objective - the high ground of Pilckem Ridge.

The German Reserve Divisions reached the Yser Canal and established bridgeheads on the west bank at Steenstraat and the lock at Het Sas. A gap in the Allied front line was created as a result of the French withdrawal. The route to Ypres was open.

The left wing of the British Second Army sector (at St. Julien) was not directly attacked. However, as a result of the French withdrawing on their immediate left, the rear of 13th Battalion of 1st Canadian Division was in danger of being exposed. This battalion, together with some French troops, formed a flank on the left wing of the British sector along the St. Julien-Poelcappelle road.

They put up a stubborn defence to hinder the progress of the German Reserve Division on the left wing of the German attack.

By midnight on 22$^{nd}$ April the Allies had lost significant ground in the north part of the Ypres Salient. At about 8.30pm the German infantry stopped advancing holding an advantageous position on the high ground of Pilckem Ridge. At this point, German artillery subjected Ypres and its surrounding area to heavy artillery bombardment during the evening. This hindered the Allies as they attempted to bring reinforcements into the area overnight.

**Total Canadian casualties were about 340.**

**On April 24$^{th}$., - May 4$^{th}$., 1915 – St. Julien. Part of 2$^{nd}$. Ypres.**

The Battle of St. Julien began with the second gas attack by the Germans at Ypres (Belgium). The front line of Apex was held by Brigadier-General A.W. Currie and Brigadier-General R.E.W. Turner. At 4 A.M. on 24 April 1915 the German bombardment began, at the same time, they released chlorine gas in the direction of the lines held by 1st Canadian Division Lieutenant-General E.A.H. Alderson.

Even under the extreme conditions caused by the gas, the Canadian battalions momentarily halted the initial waves of Germans.

Fighting by those units allowed the Canadian brigades to move to positions along the Gravenstafel Ridge.

At the same time, the Germans launched an attack between Kitcheners Wood and Keerselare. In spite their best efforts, the Canadian front-line units only gave little to the German attack, and they withdrew to positions along the Gravenstafel Ridge.

In the meantime, several British battalions arrived in the Canadian sector to help reinforce the lines and new defensive positions were gradually established.

The 2nd Brigade, on the far right of the Canadian line, still held part of its original front line at the end of the day on the 24th of April.

In the morning of the 25th, a British brigade launched a counter-attack in the area between Kitcheners Wood and St-Julien. The attack solidified the line causing the Germans to commit troops that were planned to conduct an attack of their own in this area.

The Canadian units held the line for most of the day but by evening, the German attack forced the Canadians back behind Gravenstafel. The remaining troops of the Brigade were relieved in place by a British unit.

The remainder of the Canadian Division was gradually relieved in place by British units with most Canadians out of the line on the 26th of April.

That brought an end to the fighting for the infantry battalions of the 1st Canadian Division in the Battle of St-Julien, although British units continue to fight in the area for several more days. The Headquarters of the 1st Canadian Division remained in command of its area on the 2nd. of May and Canadian Artillery batteries supported British formations until 19 June 1915.

This battle was the first time poison gas was used on the Western Front and also the first time that a former colonial force (The 1st. Canadian Division) defeated a European power – the German Empire.

The Allies reported that 5,000 soldiers had been killed and 14,000 wounded

May 8th., to 13th., 1915 –

## Battle of Frezenberg Ridge – Part 2 of 2nd Ypres

The Germans field artillery moved forward with three army corps opposite the 27th. and 28th. Divisions on the Frezenberg ridge. The German attack began on May 8th. with a bombardment of the 83rd Brigade in trenches on the forward side of the ridge. The first and second assaults were repelled by the survivors. But the third German assault pushed the Allied troops back. Although the 80th. Brigade repulsed the attack, the 84th. Brigade was pushed back; this left a 3.2 km gap in the line.

The Germans were prevented from advancing further by Princess Patricia's Canadian Light Infantry's counter-attacks and a night move by the 10th Brigade. The PPCLI held the line at a steep cost, having their 700-man force was reduced to 150, who were in no shape to fight.

## Battle of Festubert May 17th. – 25th., 1915

A 60-hour bombardment before the Battle of Festubert began on the morning of 13 May 1915, when 433 howitzers and guns began a systematic working over of German defences on a frontage of 5,000 yards extending north from the village itself.

The fire was slow and deliberate (just 50 rounds per gun every 24 hours) in keeping with Haig's desire that effects on the German defences could be observed. The 6-inch guns fired on the German parapet while 4.5-inch guns shelled support and communication trenches.

Field guns bombarded wire entanglements and dropped harassing fire in the form of shrapnel shells into communication trenches. The fire was originally to last just 36 hours but extended another 24 at the request of one of the assault divisions. The 1st Corps used just over 100,000 rounds of ammunition in total.

The infantry launched their first assault on the night of 15-16 May 1915. The 2nd Division attacked at midnight.

The 7th Division was scheduled to join in on the right, attacking on a frontage of half a mile during which time the 2nd Division would again advance to the second objective which was the line of la Quinque Rue, a road running northeast out of Festubert.

Festubert marked the first British night attack of the war, and it was partially successful, the right brigade achieving the German breastwork soundlessly, but on the northern flank, the planned demonstration by the Lahore Division (who fired small-arms in an attempt to divert the Germans' attention) only managed to alert the enemy that an operation was underway, and both of the two assault brigades on the left were driven back by heavy fire.

The 7th Division began its attack at 3:15 a.m., The divisions tried twice to tie their flanks in during 16 May, but failed. Nonetheless, the Germans discarded any notion of regaining their lost trenches, and the divisional commander of the 14th Infantry Division pulled back on a 3,000 yard frontage. They formed a new line of resistance 500 yards behind la Quinque Rue which for several days the British were unable to identify with accuracy, opposite Festubert.

The German withdrawal was seen as evidence that resistance was breaking down and at mid-morning on May 17th. General Haig gave fresh orders to the 1st Corps to consolidate along la Quinque Rue, with brigade commanders permitted to continue pressing if opportunities presented themselves. The 3rd Canadian Brigade was at the disposal of the 1st Corps.

The Corps Commander named the 3rd Canadian Brigade to assault on the 7th Division's front; immediately on the left the 2nd Division would attack with the 4th Guards Brigade.

The Canadian assault called for two companies of the 14th Battalion on the left and one from the 16th Battalion on the right to attack eastward to the road and the orchard beyond. The battle promised new challenges:

The Battalions were to attack over a country they had never seen before, and depended on guides from the troops in line, rather than on the map.

The Canadian attack did not go forward until 5:25 p.m. by which time the Guards Brigade had already been halted by German machine-guns - scarcely touched by the British artillery due to their positions still not having been precisely located.

The German withdrawal was seen as evidence that resistance was breaking down and the army commander put the 3rd Canadian Brigade at the disposal of the 1st Corps. The 14th Battalion attacked with "A" and "C" Company forward; to their left the Guards Brigade, and to their right the 16th Battalion.

Told not to expect serious opposition, they moved into the former German front line, and set off immediately into heavy shell and machine gun fire with an officer from 1/8 Royal Scots as a guide, aiming at a position known as "The Orchard" as their objective.

Lieutenant-Colonel Burland, in charge of the assault companies, ordered the line to halt in the face of the devastating German fire and attempt to dig in.

"Both the attack and the withdrawal were made under trying conditions - in darkness, under constant fire, and across water-logged country seamed with deep ditches and old trenches." Some 65 other ranks were casualties, most of them fatal, including 18 NCOs. The 14th Battalion remained in support trenches until May 22nd. under constant shellfire, losing 75 other ranks killed and wounded, as well as one officer killed and another wounded while attached to the 13th Battalion.

The Montrealers of the 14th Battalion had met fire from the same un-located machine-guns that had harried the Guards and were diverted south, halted about 400 yards from their jumping-off trenches. The 16th Battalion (Canadian Scottish) had an adventure just assembling for the attack. In the early hours of 17 May, after the 3rd Brigade had received its orders attaching it to the 7th Division, the battalions had deployed in assembly trenches while the battalion C.O.s assembled for a brigade conference.

The Brigadier desired to concentrate the four Canadian battalions at a cluster of houses known as Indian Village, but no roads connected the current billet site, requiring a cross-country march. Reconnaissance parties from each battalion returned after the brigade had been stood down, and at 8:00 p.m. the four battalions marched five miles through steady rain to new billets, a trek of two hours.

The last troops were able to turn in by 1:00 a.m. on May 18th., and new orders arrived at 4:00 a.m., with demands that the brigade return to Indian Village. Officers of the 16th noted that the men were "dead tired" when they set out at 6:45 a.m., and the trip, cross-country, took until 4:00 p.m.

It was a complex plan, and a number of other variables threatened to unravel things. In addition to the inaccurate maps, printed upside down and with poor iconography, the frontal attack was to be made over ground laced with deep drainage ditches and abandoned German and Allied breastworks. No. 4 Company also had to rendezvous with a British staff officer somewhere in Festubert, as he was the only person who knew where the start line for their attack was going to be.

Not surprisingly, the plan began unravelling from the outset. As the three companies began moving toward the objective in extended formation, the Germans zeroed in on the troops with heavy artillery fire. Most of the shells fell on the left and centre of the Montrealers, which caused them to begin shrinking to the right across the front of Captain William Rae's advancing No. 2 Company. All three companies became hopelessly entangled and lost all cohesion, so that finally the officers just herded the soldiers into hodgepodge clusters and led them onward. Finally the attackers were forced to ground by the withering fire about 500 yards short of the orchard with men scattered on either side of la Quinque rue.

No. 4 Company was heavily shelled while passing through Festubert, and broke into small parties to run the gauntlet.

Their escort, a soldier from The Queen's Own Cameron Highlanders, assured them of the staff officer's presence, but he never made the rendezvous.

The map was of no use in locating either the objective of the orchard, or a communication trench that the company was to use for cover in its advance. The company commander ordered his men to drop their packs and take a chance on finding the trench, which was soon discovered on setting out. They advanced to link up with the survivors of the frontal assault, to be informed of its failure.

The 3rd Canadian Brigade did manage to reduce a gap between the positions of the 2nd and 7th British Divisions. Relief companies of the 16th Battalion worked through the night in driving rain to consolidate the gains and create a continuous line. The Germans, for their part, credited their heavy artillery fire for stopping the Allied attacks cold.

On the night of 18-19 May, the 2nd Canadian Brigade moved up on the 3rd Brigade's right and took over positions as part of a series of reliefs in which the 2nd and 7th Divisions were replaced by the 51st (Highland) and 1st Canadian Divisions. The latter two were grouped tactically under the command of General Alderson, and designated "Alderson's Force".

The Germans were also busy reorganizing, and all available reserves were being rushed forward to shore up a situation seen as precarious. Company and battalion sized units marched and even came by rail and took over positions opposite the 1st Canadian Division and 2nd British Division.

On 20 May, the 2nd and 3rd Canadian Brigades were ordered to make a fresh assault at. The 3rd Brigade was to simultaneously secure half a mile of that new enemy front line and capture The Orchard, now christened "Canadian Orchard" . The Indian Corps was to again attempt to secure Ferme du Bois, and a comprehensive artillery program by every gun and howitzer in the 1st Army was to precede the operation.

The attack on the 20th began in broad daylight, the bombardment starting at 4:00 p.m. and the attack launching at 7:45 p.m. The 16th Battalion (Canadian Scottish) and 15th Battalion (48th Highlanders of Canada) were designated by the 3rd Brigade as the assault battalions.

Lieutenant-Colonel Leckie of the 16th protested the order, attacking over open ground, and with only a single company detailed to attack Canadian Orchard. Brigadier-General Turner replied that the British felt, after the experiences at Aubers Ridge, that night operations restricted the ability of commanders to control troop movements and despite the disadvantages of exposure to accurate enemy fire, there was an advantage to be gained by attacking in daylight.

No. 3 Company managed to reach the orchard, and despite the enemy being well dug-in, the defenders were surprised and evicted, putting the Canadian Scottish within 100 yards of the main German trenches. The attempts to attack were turned back by heavy fire and belts of barbed wire. The Canadian Scottish had made the deepest penetration of any unit of the British 1st Army during the Battle of Festubert, and Canadian Orchard remained in Allied hands until the German offensives in the spring of 1918.

The 15th Battalion had as fruitless an attack as No. 1 Company of the Canadian Scottish, and the Highlanders suffered heavy casualties attacking over open ground into the teeth of machine-guns and watchful German artillery observers. Despite using short 20-yard dashes, many men were hit, and though they gained the relative safety of the North Breastwork, they were stopped 100 yards beyond it.

The 8th and 10th Battalions had moved into the line on the night of May 19th. as the 2nd Brigade assumed its position in the battle line. The trenches were found to be in poor condition, and unburied corpses and untended wounded men were found in abundance.

Brigadier-General Arthur Currie, like the C.O. of the Canadian Scottish, protested vehemently when the order to attack was received. Originally scheduled for 21 May, then cancelled, the attack order was received from 1st Army with less than five hours notice on May 20th.

General Currie requested a day's postponement to "make better preparations" but Alderson would only confirm the order. Currie noted it was his first major difference of opinion with a superior, and he was left "angry and bitter" about being forced to take an action he knew to be wrong.

As with the 15th Battalion's attack, the attack of the 10th did not go well - "doomed to failure before it started" in the words of the Army's official historian.

In an afternoon reconnaissance Brig.-Gen. Currie had been unable to identify his objective, which was shown as a small circle on the map. (A major disadvantage of this method of designating positions was the use of the same symbol regardless of the nature of the feature to be identified. To confuse matters further, the Festubert trench map was full of inaccuracies, with errors in position amounting to as much as 450 yards. Furthermore, it was printed upside-down, with the north at the bottom of the sheet and the east on the left.)

Currie therefore asked for the attack to be postponed until next day, but was refused. Even his expected fire support was reduced. The original artillery plan had included a blasting of K.5 by two 9.2-inch howitzers, but this was cancelled lest the necessary withdrawal of Canadians from the danger zone near such a bombardment should alert the Germans, who from Aubers Ridge could look right into the First Army's positions. The 10th Battalion's attacking party cleared the communication trench of enemy for 100 yards, but as the brigade bombers emerged in single file into the open they came under a storm of fire from machine-guns on built-up positions which had been unharmed by our artillery. Seeing the leaders all shot down, the company commander halted the suicidal advance and ordered the gains made good.

There was no record of the number of casualties in the 10th Battalion attack, but a renewed attack was immediately called for dawn on 21 May, then postponed until after dark to allow for a proper bombardment.

To that end, a bombardment of three and a half hours, beginning at 5:00 p.m. and in the words of the Army historian, the bombardment was "woefully ineffective." The field guns had been dispersed across the front, and ammunition shortages required them to fire shrapnel shells, comparatively ineffective against the German strongpoints as opposed to the heavier guns of the siege batteries.

Counter-battery artillery fire was still in its infancy and German guns, heavier and with ample supplies of shells, were able to respond by shelling the Canadian infantry heavily.

The 2nd Brigade's assault was made by the same two companies of the 10th Battalion, together with the 1st Brigade's grenade company, carrying 500 bombs. From breaches cut in the sides of the approach trench half the force broke out to the left, half to the right. The former, advancing across 200 yards of open ground towards K.5, was quickly cut to pieces by machine-gun fire. The right-hand party, however, attacking the western face of the salient, met less resistance and drove the enemy out of 400 yards of his front line. During the night the Germans attempted several counter-attacks, which the Canadian garrison, reinforced by a company of the 5th Battalion, drove off. Then, with the coming of daylight on the 22nd, enemy guns began a heavy bombardment of their lost position. Large portions of the breastworks were blown away and the Allied occupants wiped out. Before midday Currie withdrew his men from all but 100 yards of the newly occupied line. The 10th Battalion had by then suffered casualties of 18 officers and 250 other ranks.

On the morning of 22 May, General Haig visited General Alderson to express his dissatisfaction at the failure of the Canadians to achieve their objectives and insist that the Germans be pushed out of their positions.

At an Army conference next morning he ordered a thorough reconnaissance of the enemy's positions before planning the next attack, which would be a combined effort by the Canadian Division and the 47th Division on its right to reduce the German position.

The final Canadian actions at Festubert were fought by "Seely's Detachment", which relieved the 2nd Brigade on May 24th.

Following the carnage of the 2nd Battle of Ypres, and in response to the desperate need for infantry, the cavalrymen volunteered to serve in France, and moved from their training camps in the United Kingdom on May 4th., numbering about 1,500 men, leaving behind their horses with British Yeomanry units.

The British attacked at 6:30 p.m. on May 25th. north of the Givenchy-Chapelle St. Roch road and two battalions advanced 400 yards to take the German forward and support trenches on a 1,000 yard front, suffering 980 casualties in the process.

On May 31st., the 1st Canadian Division began a shift to its right in order to take over a new sector at Givenchy, to the immediate north of the canal, as part of a 1st Army reorganization, in the wake of Sir John French's decision on May 25th. to stop the Festubert fighting and attempt new missions to assist the French offensive. Major offensives were out of the question due to ammunition shortages.

Festubert had been a frustrating experience. Substantial gains had been looked for but not achieved, and in the lower echelons, where the Army's role of easing pressure on the French was little appreciated, few could readily share the Commander-in-Chief's view of an objective attained.

In the course of the battle Canadians had assaulted on five separate days, to advance their line an average distance of 600 yards across a one-mile front. Except for the capture of a bit of German defences at K.5 their attacks had not reached the enemy line. In doing this they had suffered 2468 casualties.

The Canadian Division had returned to action a little more than two weeks after losing half its' fighting strength at Ypres.

Once again the superiority of the German artillery had decided the issue.

The enemy's organized shelling of the front line and support trenches prevented the assembly of troops within reasonable assaulting distance of their objective and kept reinforcements from coming forward to exploit initial gains.

The original history of the C.E.F. described the battle at Festubert as "the most unsatisfactory engagement" involving Canadians of the entire war. Half the infantry who fought there had been fresh from reinforcement camps in the U.K. and barely arrived from Canada, thrown into action just three weeks after the horrifying losses of 2nd Ypres.

The 1st Division lost 93 officers, 1 in 5 belonging to the 10th Battalion, though that battalion lost less than a tenth of the 2,230 other ranks. Over establishment early in May, the 10th Battalion was at half strength on May 30th.. The 16th Battalion had lost 277 men, including 6 officers, 3 of them dead. No. 3 Company had been reduced to just 56 effectives

**Battle of Bellewaerde Ridge – 24th -25th of May, 1915.**

The Canadian Division was successfully relieved at the start of May, after suffering about 6,000 losses, though fighting in the Ypres Salient continued for three weeks more, the only Canadian infantry unit to remain engaged was the PPCLI, fighting with the 80th Brigade of the British 27th Division. The Patricias had served at St. Eloi from January 7th. to March 23rd. 1915, carrying out a local attack on 28 February with about 100 men, destroying 30 yards of German trench for a loss of 5 dead and 9 wounded. They moved into the Ypres Salient on April 9th.when their division relieved the French 17th Division, occupying positions in front of Polygon Wood.

When the 2nd Battle of Ypres opened, the Patricias suffered 80 casualties from enemy shellings. As the battle continued, General Plumer was given command of all troops in the Ypres area, and on the night of May 3rd & 4th. he ordered a general withdrawal to new positions. The Patricias fell back to Bellewaarde Ridge, half a mile northeast of Hooge, into incomplete and shallow trenches. Shelling and machine-gun fire caused 122 more casualties.

A bombardment along the 5th Corps front signalled another German attack, and three converging assaults had been ordered in an attempt to reduce the Salient.

The 26th Reserve Corps advanced from the north against the sector Mouse Trap Farm to Frezenberg; the 27th Reserve Corps to make the central and main attack westward between Frezenberg and Bellewaarde Lake; and the 15th Corps to break through north-westward between Bellewaarde and Zillebeke Lakes. The 27th and 28th British Divisions were under attack by at least six German divisions.

As a preliminary, in three gas attacks on May 5th. the 15th Corps had captured Hill 60. The brunt of the main onslaught on the 8th fell on the 28th Division's 83rd and 84th Brigades holding Frezenberg Ridge.

Two assaults were beaten back, but the third overwhelmed the front line, and by mid-morning Frezenberg had fallen. Before noon the Germans had penetrated nearly a mile and were in Verlorenhoek.

They advanced no farther, but by mid-afternoon they had widened their breach of the Salient two miles and had begun rolling up the British line on either flank.

In their positions on Bellewaarde Ridge at the 27th Division's left the Patricias with the 80th Brigade's other front-line battalion, the 4th King's Royal Rifle Corps, on their right, held the southern shoulder of the gap. The devastating fire that the enemy concentrated on the British trenches from the Menin Road to Frezenberg obliterated whole sections of the P.P.C.L.I. front line on the forward slope of the ridge.

Two of the unit's four machine-guns were put out of action and casualties were so heavy that Major Hamilton Gault, who had taken over command of the regiment on May 5th. , ordered signallers, pioneers, orderlies and batmen forward into the support trenches.

When the Germans launched their main assault at 9:00 a.m., the Patricias' steady rifle fire drove them back on the left; but on the right the enemy gained a footing, compelling a retirement to the main defence line on the crest.

Here the battalion, reinforced by a company from the 4th Rifle Brigade, stood unflinchingly for the rest of the day, enduring repeated bombardments and beating back every German attempt to advance from the captured trenches.

During the afternoon the left flank, drawn back to face the danger from the north, was extended by reserve battalions of the 80th and 81st Brigades. These units joined the counter attacking battalions of the 85th Brigade in the centre to seal off the German encroachment. East of Mouse Trap Farm a heroic stand by the 2nd Northumberland Fusiliers, when the remainder of the 84th Brigade's front-line battalions were annihilated, held firm the northern shoulder of the gap.

On the 4th Division's front west of Mouse Trap Farm British artillery (including eight Canadian field batteries) broke up the infantry attack which followed the early morning bombardment.

When the Patricias were relieved shortly before midnight, their total trench strength was four officers and 150 men. The day's casualties totalled 392.

For the last few days of the Battle of Frezenberg Ridge (which ended on May 13th.) they joined with the 4th King's Royal Rifles, which had shared their valiant stand on Bellewaarde Ridge. On 24 May, when the Fourth Army attacked the 5th Corps, releasing a heavy concentration of chlorine along a front of 4-1/2 miles, the 27th Division was in corps reserve.

The Germans captured Mouse Trap Farm and Bellewaarde Ridge, breaking through on both sides of Bellewaarde Lake. Late on the 24th the 80th Brigade made an unsuccessful counter-attack, the Patricias being held in brigade reserve. This operation, named the Battle of Bellewaarde Ridge, ended the Battles of Ypres, 1915.

The PPCLI suffered 678 casualties during the period in action with the 27th Division from 10 April to 21 May 1915. Ypres, however, had been held.

## Second Action of Givenchy - 15th. – 16th. of June, 1915

The 3rd Battalion participants that the action at Givenchy was the most brutal and intense fighting of the war.

This was the final act of the British command that starting at Neuve Chapelle and ending with defeats at Aubers Ridge and Festubert. Seven battalions including the 1st (Western Ontario) Battalion) took part. With the Canadian Division remaining in the Bethune area after the Battle of Festubert.

They moved a few miles south to the La Bassee Canal and the village of Givenchy. The 1st Battalion held the right flank. On this occasion heavy artillery was used to eliminate the machine nests located on the parapets. As well a mine was set by Engineers to blow at Zero hour (5:45 pm, June 15th.) under the German line. From a Canadian perspective, the attack went well. The German strong point H.3 was captured and some men made it across Duck's Bill into the German trench with a Victoria Cross being captured by Lt. Frederick Campbell.

However the units on the flanks were not so successfully with the 1st Battalion reversing their attack and withdrawing back to the crater, assisted by the 2nd and 3rd Battalions.. They had 386 casualties, 46% of their strength.

Despite the failure, orders were issued by the 1st Canadian Brigade to renew the attack. The 3rd Battalion attacked 4:45 pm June 16 after a two hour artillery attack. "The attack seemed from every angle one viewed it, as futile and hopeless. The attackers had no supporting fire. They were shot down as they climbed over the parapet. None of them got over 25 yards, except perhaps a few who were trapped in the sap and could nothing but lie low and await a chance to return".

The 3rd Battalion lost 115 men, killed and wounded, at Givenchy. Total Canadian losses for two days fighting were 802, including 306 killed. British losses totalled 3,009. The nonsense was called off early on the 19th with the 1st Canadian Division heading north to the Ploegsteert Woods area of Belgium.

After the battle, as in all intense battles, bodies were left on the battleground as it was much too dangerous to remove the dead and wounded from the active battlefield. The same German machine guns and accurate artillery that were reasonable for the disappointing defeat at Givenchy and H.2, H.3 meant the casualties remained where they lay. However on June 18, occurred an amazing and brave deed by the 7th (British Columbia) Battalion commander at the time by Lt-Col Victor W. Odium took place.

At night volunteer party brought in bodies of 52 men of 1st Brigade from in front of trenches at Ducks Bill. Buried them behind parapet. Lieut H.H. Owen brought in 1 wounded man who had been out between lines 2 days. Lieut R.F.E. Buscombe killed in early morning of 18th while burying 1st Brigade dead. Collected arms discarded by 1st Brigade.

**The Battle of Loos – 25th. September – 8th. of October, 1915**

The Battle of Loos took place from September 25th – October 8th., 1915 in France on the Western Front, during the First World War. It was the biggest British attack of 1915 and the first time the British used poison gas and the first engagement of New Army units. The French and British tried to break through the German defences in Artois and Champagne and restore a war of movement.

Despite improved methods, more ammunition and better equipment, the Franco-British attacks were contained by the German armies, except for local losses of ground. British casualties at Loos were about twice as high as German losses

Canadian troops repelled 21 German counter-attacks to maintain the Allies' hold on their positions on Hill 70.

In total, about 9,000 Canadians and 25,000 Germans were killed or wounded during the battle.

The Battle of Hill 70 took place on September 1915, the British overran the hill during the Battle of Loos but it was recaptured by the Germans. The 1st Canadian Division artillery suffered 183 casualties and three batteries suffered direct hits.

## Action of St. Eloi Craters – 27th. March – 16th. of April, 1916

The Battle of St. Eloi Craters was fought from March 27th., to April 16th.,1916 during the First World War. The Belgian terrain was wet and swampy, and was the first major engagement for the 2nd Canadian division. It was a long battle and a disaster for Canada and the Allies..

By mid-1916, armies on both sides of the First World War were using mining as a part of trench warfare. Tunnels were dug across the battlefield and explosives planted under enemy positions. The tunnelers would retreat and blow them up. The fields were marked with craters from these underground explosions. Thus the name "St. Eloi Craters."

In early 1916, the Canadian Corps' 2nd Division was sent to fight Germans at St. Eloi. The Canadians had no time to prepare for the attack. The intent was for the British troops to strike and then for the Canadians to take over and hold the line.

The fighting started at 4:15 a.m. on March 27th. with heavy fire. Six British mines were set off one after the other, shaking the earth "like the sudden outburst of a volcano" and filling the sky with yellow smoke and debris, according to the Canadian Expeditionary Force's war record. The explosion was heard in England. The German trenches collapsed.

The British soldiers rose from their positions attacked, quickly capturing three craters and the third German line. For several days, British soldiers fought hand-to-hand with Germans, and advanced until April 3rd.

The landscape being reshaped by the explosions and craters left the British were not sure where they were. Four mines blew up so close to each other that the craters formed an impassable lake that was 15 m deep and 55 m across. (It later became a recreational fishing lake for a summer cottage).

British troops fought from inside the craters, crouching in mud or standing in waist-deep water, unable to sit. High winds, sleet and mud

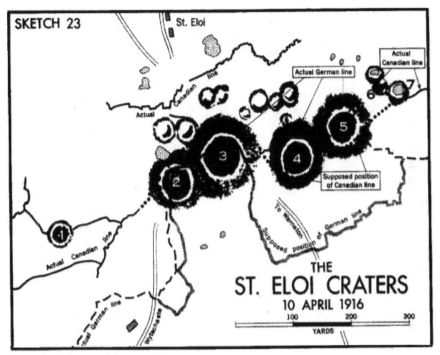

created nightmarish conditions.

Hundreds of men were killed on either side in a week of constant shooting. The exhausted British troops were relieved by the Canadian troops at 3 a.m. on April 4th.

A ST. ELOI CRATER

A picture taken three years after the explosion of the St. Eloi mines shows one of the water-filled craters

The excited Canadians were eager to do battle but found a shortage of steel helmets, machine guns and defensive positions. The 2nd Canadian Pioneer Battalion improved the defences and attempted to drain the trenches of water. At the same time the entire front line remained under constant bombardment on April 4th and 5th., with hundreds more troops being killed.

**One Canadian soldier wrote to his wife that *"we were walking on dead soldiers"* as they tried to advance. *Wounded and traumatized men streamed back to the medical officers. Some had been fighting standing in cold water and mud for 48 straight hours, and officers had been awake for 100 hours."***

At 3:30 a.m. on April 6th., 1916, two German battalions attacked down the ruins of the main road. The confused Canadian troops having lost communication with each other were quickly repelled. As the sun rose over the wasteland, the Germans had recaptured all of the ground taken from them at the start of the battle.

The Canadians fought back with bombs but could not make advances in the heavy rain.

Troops attempted to recapture two craters but got stuck in the mud and were shot dead. A group of Canadians recaptured Craters 6 and 7, but thought they were in Craters 4 and 5. In the confusion they were cut off and left open to the German onslaught.

As night fell on April 8th., 1916, the Canadians attacked but were stopped again by German fire. Rain made impassable mud of the battlefield. Germans attacked the next day but were likewise repelled. The Canadian leadership had little idea which craters they held and which were held by Germans. The leadership did not know what was happening at the front, as disoriented Canadians pinned down by artillery shells could not relay messages. Even the carrier pigeons were dead.

Both sides shot at each other in the miserable conditions of the craters for another two weeks. More than 1,370 Canadians were killed or wounded, along with about 480 Germans. On April 16th., the divisional headquarters ordered the battle stopped.

Still, the German attack continued with tear gas with the exhausted Canadians still fighting off the enemy. On April 17th. A German night raid through pounding rain drove the Canadians back further. Mud stopped Canadians guns from firing. Half of the remaining men in the craters surrendered to the Germans, and the rest crawled away.

The Battle of St. Eloi's Craters ended with the Germans again in control of the battlefield.


**Battle of Mount Sorrel - 2nd. – 13th. of June, 1916**

Thousands of Canadians were killed and wounded in the fighting, from June 2nd. – 13th., 1916, for this Mount Sorrel in the Ypres Salient in Belgium.

In early 1916, the 3rd Division of the Canadian Corps defended Mount Sorrel, a 30-metre hill overlooking the city of Ypres and the important road between Ypres and the town of Menin. Heavy rain and constant shelling left the ground a soggy mess.

On June2nd., German troops attacked the Canadians and the Allied trenches were blown apart, killing hundreds of Canadian troops and blasting apart their garrisons. The 4th Canadian Mounted Rifles was nearly wiped out — 90 per cent of the regiment's men were killed or injured. Of the 702 soldiers in the regiment who defended against the German attack, only 76 were unhurt by the end of the battle.

The Germans also attacked from below, detonating mines they had positioned beneath the Canadian positions. German infantry crossed the plains advancing up Mount Sorrel.

Major General Malcolm Mercer, the 3rd Division's commander, was killed and Brigadier General V.A.S. Williams, commander of the Division's 8th Brigade, was wounded and taken prisoner. Both leaders were hit by the German assault while were on a reconnaissance mission.

German forces overwhelmed the Canadian troops and captured Mount Sorrel along with Hill 61and Hill 62. The Canadians tried to retake the hills on June 3rd. The plan was to attack under cover of darkness at about 2 a.m., but the attack did not start until after dawn and the Germans repelled the attack.

The Germans additionally captured Hooge, a village on the main road. They were now well-positioned to attack the city of Ypres itself.

The Allies attempted to reclaim Mount Sorrel, but troops and supplies were in short supply as the Allies were also planning the Somme Offensive in France. The British 2nd Calvary Brigade came to the aid of the Canadians.

Starting on June 9th., Allied forces attacked the German hilltop positions with artillery.

At 1:30 a.m. on June 13th., the Allies followed with an infantry attack under the cover of a smoke screen. Fighting in the dark, amid flares of light from the heavy attack, the Canadian and British soldiers pushed through the wind and rain to recapture the Mount Sorrel.

"The first Canadian deliberately planned attack in any force had resulted in an unqualified success," said the British Official History of the war.

Between June 2nd and 14th., more than 1,100 Canadians were killed at Mount Sorrel, with more than 2,000 men missing. Thousands more were injured.

In total, 8,430 Canadian troops were killed, wounded or reported missing. The Germans suffered 5,765 men killed, injured or missing.

Today, a monument known as Mount Sorrel sits by the Sanctuary Wood Museum near Ypres.

The inscription reads: "Here at Mount Sorrel and on the line from Hooge to St. Eloi, the Canadian Corps fought in the defence of Ypres April-August 1916".

Mount Sorrel-Passchendale
Courtesy of Wikipedia

**Pozieres Ridge (Mouquet Farm) – 1st. – 3rd. of September, 1916**

The 1st Division held the whole of the Corps front three thousand yards of battered trenches running westward along the Pozieres Ridge from the boundary with the Fourth Army to a point 700 yards west of Mouquet Farm, The Australians' final attempt to capture Mouquet Farm was made on September 3rd, by their 13th Brigade, which had the 13th Battalion, of the relieving 3rd Canadian Brigade, temporarily under command.

The attack, while failing to secure the farm, gained 300 yards of Fabeck Graben, a German trench running north-eastward towards Courcelette. In attempting to extend this holding two companies of the Canadian battalion suffered 322 casualties.

The relief of the Australians was completed on the morning of the 5th, and for three more days the 3rd Canadian Brigade continued to hold under heavy fire and frequent counter-attack more than two thousand yards of line, including the captured portion of Fabeck Graben. The brigade's 970 casualties in this period gave it good reason to remember its first tour of duty at the Somme.

Early on September 8th., during a relief by the 2nd Brigade, the Germans regained the almost obliterated section of Fabeck Graben. Next day the Canadians improved their positions, when the 2nd Canadian Battalion captured a portion of a German trench about 500 yards long south of the Cambrai road. In gaining and retaining its objective (and thereby earning the congratulations of the Commander-in-Chief) the battalion owed much to the valour of one of its junior N.C.Os.—Corporal Leo Clarke. While clearing a continuation of the newly-captured trench during the construction of a permanent block on the battalion flank, most of the members of his small bombing party were killed or wounded and their supply of grenades was exhausted. Clarke was building a temporary barricade when an enemy party of twenty, led by two officers, counterattacked down the trench.

Coolly the corporal fought them off. Twice he emptied into the Germans his own revolver, and then two abandoned enemy rifles. He shot and killed an officer who had bayoneted him in the leg, and he is credited with having killed or wounded at least sixteen enemies before the rest turned in flight. Then he shot down four more of the fleeing Germans, and captured a fifth-the sole enemy survivor. His courageous action brought Corporal Clarke the first of two Victoria Crosses to be won by his battalion. He was killed five weeks later, before the award was announced.

# Flers-Courcelette - 15<sup>th</sup> – 22<sup>nd</sup>. of September, 1916

The Battle of Flers-Courcelette, the two-army assault launched by Sir Douglas Haig on September 15<sup>th</sup>., was fought on a wider front as the two villages are three miles apart, but the battle area extended for ten miles from Combles, on the French left, to Thiepval, overlooking the east bank of the Ancre.

General Rawlinson's Fourth Army, delivered the main attack with three corps, with objectives Flers and the neighbouring villages of Morval, Lesboeufs and Gueudecourt, all of which were defended by the German Third Position.

It was hoped that a breakthrough here would open the way for cavalry to advance on Bapaume.

Bapaume, France is situated between Artois and Somme, both important places for both sides. The Germans occupied the town in 1914. It changed hands three times towards war end. In February 1917 the German forces withdrew several kilometres to the north and destroyed all the infrastructure before they left so it would be of no use to the British.

The Reserve Army's task was to protect the left flank, and to attack with the Canadian Corps to secure in the neighbourhood of Courcelette points of observation over the Third Position. Two innovations were expected to give considerable support to the assault-a creeping barrage, which the artillery had only recently adopted, and the employment of a completely new engine of war, the tank. The designation, "land-cruiser" or "land-ship" used in the experimental stage was changed to "tank", and rumours that these odd creations were water-wagons intended for the Middle East or snow-ploughs for the Russian front were not discouraged. The model that was soon to appear in battle (the Mark I) was 261 feet long with a six-foot "tail" it was almost 14 feet wide and about 71 feet high. Fully equipped it weighed 28 tons. A six cylinder, 105-horsepower Daimler engine gave it a maximum speed of 3.7 miles an hour. It could cross a trench ten feet wide. Tanks were designated "male" or "female" according to armament.

The "male" was armed with two six-pounder guns and four Hotchkiss machine-guns for destroying enemy machine-gun posts; the "female" carried only machine-guns -five Vickers and one Hotchkiss—for employment against enemy personnel. The crew, provided by the Heavy Branch Machine Gun Corps. (later renamed the Tank Corps), numbered one officer and seven men.

The first tanks were shipped to France in mid-August, and early in September a small training centre was set up near Abbeville for the two newly formed companies (each comprising 25 machines) allotted to the forthcoming battle. There was time only for crews to acquire skill in driving and gunnery, and very little opportunity for infantry and tanks to train together.

The July battles had exposed the fallacy of trusting to the preliminary bombardment to wipe out all opposition. To the end of the Somme battles unit and formation commanders were to be governed by the training instructions issued by General Headquarters in May: ". . . . in many instances experience has shown that to capture a hostile trench a single line of men has usually failed, two lines have generally failed but sometimes succeeded, three lines have generally succeeded but sometimes failed, and four or more lines have usually succeeded."

Of the forty-nine tanks available, the Reserve Army's share of seven were allotted to General Turner. This Canadian armour was organized in two detachments of three tanks each, one tank kept in reserve. The right-hand detachment, with the 4th Canadian Brigade, had orders to advance at top speed astride the Bapaume road through a lane in the artillery barrage, and engage hostile machine-guns in Martinpuich and the sugar factory.

The tanks supporting the 6th Brigade on the left were to move up behind the barrage and "cover the left flank of the advancing Infantry and assist in mopping up." On reaching the sugar factory they would "attack any machine guns there or in Courcelette that they can deal with".

Five infantrymen were assigned to each tank, to walk ahead and remove casualties from its path. Zero hour was at 6:20 a.m. on

September 15th., and promptly the guns standing almost wheel to wheel in Sausage Valley behind Pozieres joined in the tremendous bombardment that burst from the mile upon mile' of batteries of all calibres massed along the front.

The mechanical roar of the tanks as they ground their way forward added an unfamiliar sound. The attack went well.

The artillery had crushed opposition in the German front line trenches, which were taken in fifteen minutes. On the Canadian right the three assaulting battalions of the 4th Brigade were on their objectives by seven o'clock, the 21st Battalion taking 145 prisoners out of the ruins of the sugar factory. Half an hour later the 6th Brigade reported success west of the road.

The presence of the tanks encouraged many Germans to surrender, and brought from some of these bitter criticism that it was "not war but bloody butchery". On the whole, however, the armour in its initial action failed to carry out the tasks assigned to it (though one tank, besides inflicting both physical and moral damage on the enemy, laid telephone wire from the forward infantry positions to the rear).

All six tanks with the Canadians, either through becoming stuck or breaking down, were put out of action before or during the attack, in four cases as a result of shellfire. One failed to cross the start line; and of the other five, only one reached its objective. Of the 32 tanks on the Fourth Army's start line at zero hour, only ten got fully forward to help the infantry win their objectives.

The rest bellied down or failed mechanically (for they had not been designed for such heavily cratered ground, and many miles of trial and demonstration had almost worn them out before the battle) or destroyed or damaged by artillery fire.

The tactical employment of armour had received little study. It seems a questionable procedure to have distributed the machines piecemeal along the battle front, thereby removing them from the tank company commanders' control. Properly coordinated action of artillery, tanks and infantry was still to be learned.

In reporting on the action General Turner, while forecasting that mopping up "will, in future, be the chief role of these engines", hinted at greater possibilities. "A portion of the tanks", he wrote, "should however be sent through to the final objective with the object of increasing the enemy's demoralization and keeping him on the run.

The Commander-in Chief was highly pleased with the performance of the new weapon, and four days after the battle he asked the War Office for a thousand tanks. Senior German commanders, on the other hand, were so little impressed with the tank that they did not—much to our advantage-immediately attempt to copy it; nor did they give due attention to the problem of anti-tank defence

## Thiepval Ridge – 26th. – 29th of September, 1916

The orders for the operation emphasized the necessity of driving the Germans from the whole crest-line to hide from enemy view our rear areas on the southern slopes Albert, and to give us observation over the valley of the upper Ancre. The 6000-yard front from Courcelette to Thiepval was divided between the Canadian Corps on the right and the 2nd Corps on the left.

The British divisions were assigned objectives that had become notorious as German strongholds since the offensive opened at the beginning of July. General Jacob's right had to take Mouquet Farm, and in subsequent stages Zollern Redoubt, and on the crest 500 yards to the rear, Stuff Redoubt, another bulwark of the old German Second Position. His task on the left was to assault Thiepval and then storm the strong Schwaben Redoubt, which overlooked the Ancre from the western tip of the ridge.

The defences which the Canadians were to break lay along a low spur projecting eastward from the main ridge. Linking up with the redoubts in the 2nd Corps' sector were three trench lines which were originally given as successive objectives to the 1st Canadian Division on the Corps left—Zollern Graben, Hessian Trench and Regina Trench, with its branching Kenora Trench. Although low reconnaissance patrols of the Royal Flying Corps had reported on the condition of the German defences in some detail, Hessian Trench, "owing to the uncertainty as to the condition of the wire in front of Regina Trench", was made the limit of General Currie's attack. The isolated Sudbury Trench formed an intermediate line to Kenora Trench, which was afterwards described as "one of the deepest and strongest trenches the men had ever seen".

Their eastward projection behind Courcelette as far as the Bapaume road became the single objective of the 2nd Division. For three days the artillery harassed the German positions, 500 tear-gas shells fired on the 24th silencing enemy mortars at Thiepval. The Reserve Army's assault was made with fresh troops, brought into the line between April 22nd., and the night of the 25th. Zero hour was 12:35 p.m.

On the 26th., a warm, sunny day. At 12:34 the massed machine-guns of both the 2nd and the Canadian Corps opened overhead fire. One minute later eight hundred, guns, howitzers and mortars put down a mighty barrage of shrapnel and high explosive as the first wave of infantry climbed the parapet.

A second wave, a mopping up party, and third and fourth waves followed (in the case of at least one battalion) at intervals of 70 to 100 yards. Brig.-Gen. Ketchen's 6th Brigade carried out the 2nd Division's attack on the right.

North-east of Courcelette the 29th Battalion reached and occupied the enemy's front trenches in ten minutes. On its left the 31st, advancing against heavy machine-gun and rifle fire, encountered a battalion of the German 72nd Regiment and achieved only limited success.

On the extreme right, next to the Bapaume road, the 28th Battalion had been charged with making a subsidiary attack supported by the only two tanks allotted to the Canadian Corps. (Of 20 tanks still fit for service, the Fourth Army had twelve in the Morval battle and six were being used against Thiepval by the 2nd Corps.) But one tank broke down before reaching the start line, and the other caught fire when a German shell exploded its ammunition.

As a result the battalion remained in its trenches. In the 1st Division's sector, the 3rd Brigade (Brig.-Gen. G. S. Tuxford) on the right assaulted with the 14th and 15th Battalions. Both immediately met heavy counter-fire from hostile batteries and suffered costly casualties from nests of German machine gunners, who having survived our barrage caught the second infantry wave as it mounted the parapet.

To escape destruction by our barrage, which was invariably concentrated on known trench lines, forward German troops were ordered to abandon their trenches whenever an assault seemed imminent, and to occupy shellholes or ditches well in front of where the attacking troops expected to find them. The 14th Battalion on the brigade right quickly advanced 400 yards to Sudbury Trench, where it took some forty prisoners; shortly after one o'clock it was on its way up the slope to the eastern end of Kenora Trench, its final objective.

On its left the 15th Battalion, having met with heavy and unexpected resistance from strong groups in no man's land, was unable to keep pace and the 31st. was also held up, particularly its left wing. Thus the men of the 14th Battalion on reaching their objective about mid-afternoon came under bitter counter-attack from both flanks. Enfiladed

With constant machine-gun fire they were subject to considerable shellfire during the rest of the day and the following night, and several times had to fight off enemy bombing parties.

Kenora Trench was to change hands twice before six o'clock on the evening of September 27th., when the terribly few survivors of a company of the 14th (which had been reinforced by two companies of the 16th Battalion) fell back halfway towards Sudbury Trench.

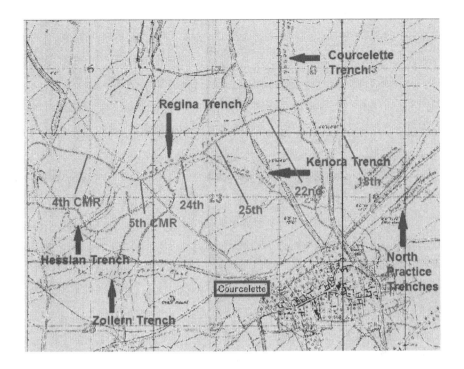

Courtesy of 18<sup>th</sup>. Batallion war Diary:

The 15th Battalion, advancing during the afternoon of the 26th in the open space not covered by Hessian or Kenora trenches, got well up the slope to within 150 yards of Regina- Trench before digging in.

In the 1st Division's left sector, the 2nd Brigade (Brig.-Gen. F. O. W. Loom's ) had to advance over the highest part of the main Thiepval Ridge. It attacked with the 5th Battalion on the right and the 8th (left), each augmented by a company of the 10th. Battalion.

Despite heavy machine-gun fire from Zollern and Stuff Redoubts and, the Mouquet Farm area, and continual shelling by the enemy's artillery, the troops reached both objectives. Neither one, however, could they completely secure. Not until next day did the Canadians clear both trenches to the corps boundary.

While the Canadian Corps had been achieving results which it considered "not unsatisfactory", over on the left, the 2nd Corps had taken all but a small corner of Thiepval and most of the western half of Zollern Graben. But the diverging directions of their attacks had left a serious gap between the two corps.

The enemy still held the commanding portions of Thiepval Ridge, and in spite of having suffered many casualties he, seemed . capable of further stout resistance. At 8.45 that evening General Gough called for the completion next day of the tasks of the 26th. Lieut.-General Byng accordingly directed the 2nd Division to secure the German front line, north-east of Courcelette and the 1st Division to attack Regina Trench and link up with General Jacob's right.

During the night of September 26-27th., the enemy opposite the 2nd Division fell back to Regina Trench. This defence line angled away from the apex of the Canadian salient to link up with the German Third Position about 1500 yards north-west of Le Sars, on the Bapaume road. Thus units and companies of the 6th Brigade were able to make satisfactory gains with little fighting. The 28th Battalion seized German positions west of the Bapaume road, while astride the Dyke road the 27th and 29th Battalions patrolled as far as the North and South Practice Trenches. Between the two Miraumont roads, however, the Germans withdraw only gradually, and under pressure. Not until 8:30 p.m. on the 27th did the 31st Battalion link up with the 3rd Brigade west of the West Miraumont road.

On the extreme left the 7th Battalion occupied Hessian Trench, putting in a block at the corps boundary. Opposite the 3rd Brigade, however, the enemy stood firm and his counter-attacks continued on the 27th. This made it impossible for the 1st Division to carry out its assault. General Byng had hoped that both Kenora and Regina Trenches would be in Canadian hands prior to an early relief of the 1st Division by the 2nd Division. But with the second loss of Kenora on the evening of the 27th the chances of this being achieved became remote.

Nevertheless the 14th Battalion, at the insistence of Brig.-Gen. Tuxford made one further attempt. At 2:00 a.m. on the 28th the Battalion, which after forty hours of continuous fighting could only assemble about 75 men, attacked through the mud and rain.

As they neared the Kenora position the Canadians were brightly illuminated by enemy flares and became easy targets for the German frontal and flanking fire.

The attack was called off, having brought the 14th Battalion's total casualties in the battle for Thiepval Ridge to ten officers and 360 other ranks. Kenora Trench was not to be taken for five more days. Regina Trench would defy capture until October 21$^{st}$, . On September 28$^{th}$., a series of Canadian reliefs brought the 4th and 5th Brigades into the line on the right and on the left the 8th Brigade replaced the 2nd, which had linked up with the 2nd Corps back towards Zollern Trench. On orders from General Turner to press the advance, early on the 28th the 19th Battalion moved forward up the Dyke road. It found the Practice Trenches abandoned, and swung eastward. When halted by fire from the strongly held Destremont Farm, just north of the Bapaume road, the Canadians succeeded in establishing a position west of the farm.

Meanwhile in the 5th Brigade's sector the 26th Battalion, attacking astride Courcelette Trench (which ran northward from the village ruins), had made two fruitless attempts to gain Regina Trench.

Late that afternoon in a coordinating move on the brigade left, the 24th Battalion had embarked on a plan of storming Regina Trench and then bombing its way eastward, while the 25th Battalion assaulted in the centre.

The effort failed, as leading parties of both battalions ran into wire entanglements uncut by our artillery, and heavy machine-gun fire mowed them down.

The 2nd Canadian Mounted Rifles, already in Hessian, began clearing it westward across the inter-corps boundary in conjunction with a frontal assault by a battalion of the 3nd Brigade.

Hand-to-hand fighting gained three hundred yards of trench. Besides losing many killed and wounded the enemy yielded up sixty prisoners.

Two German counter-attacks achieved initial but short-lived success, as Canadian bombers regained ground temporarily lost to the enemy.

Two hundred yards of Hessian Trench still in German hands fell the next afternoon to converging attacks by three battalions of the 11th Division, but all efforts failed to expel the enemy completely from the northern part of his two redoubts.

The Battle of Thiepval Ridge had ended (the official dates for the operation are September 26-28th.), though the Reserve Army had failed to capture the north-western tip of the blood-soaked feature.

North of the main ridge Regina Trench remained an untaken objective of the Canadian Corps as the month ended. General Turner had issued orders on the 29th for  Earlier that morning Canadian cavalry patrols drawn from the 19th Alberta Dragoons and the 1st Canadian Hussars had ridden out of Courcelette to probe deep into enemy territory.

Two patrols reached Regina Trench; others moving up the Bapaume road were repulsed by machine-gun fire from Destremont Farm.

Originally planned for the 29th, the operation was twice postponed 24 hours to allow the artillery to deal more effectively with the enemy's defences, and because the 5th Brigade, as reported in appreciations by battalion commanders, was "too exhausted and too few in numbers" (its fighting strength being only 1134) Across the Reserve Army's front territorial gains had brought a general straightening of the line as had been intended, the greatest progress being on the left, where the 2nd Corps had advanced 2000 yards through Thiepval to Hessian Trench.

On General Gough's right, the Fourth Army had taken Destremont Farm and closed on Le Sars (midway between Pozieres and Bapaume).

# Le Transloy Ridges (Captureof Eaucourt l'Abbaye – 1st. – 18th. of October, 1916.

On Sept. 21st., after the battle of Flers–Courcelette, Hindenburg ordered that the Somme front was to have priority in the west for troops. During September, the Germans had sent another thirteen fresh divisions to the British sector and scraped up troops wherever they could be found.

The German artillery had fired 213 train-loads of field artillery shells and 217 train-loads of heavy artillery ammunition, yet the début of the tank, the defeat at Thiepval and the 130,000 casualties suffered by the armies on the Somme in September, had been severe blows to German morale.

German artillery on the Somme slowly improved in its effect, when Gallwitz centralised fire and used aircraft reinforcements for artillery observation, which increased the accuracy and efficiency of bombardments.

The 2nd Army had been starved of reinforcements in mid-August, to replace exhausted divisions in the 1st Army and plans for a counter-stroke had been abandoned for lack of troops.

Reinforcements for the Somme front in September began to reduce the German inferiority in guns and aircraft. Field artillery reduced its barrage frontage from 400–200 yd per battery and increased its accuracy by using one air artillery flight per division.

As the Germans had been pushed out of their original defences, new positions were established based on principles of depth, dispersal and camouflage, rather than continuous lines of trenches.

Rigid defence of the front-line continued but with as few soldiers as possible, relying on the firepower of machine-guns firing from behind the front-line and from the flanks. The area behind the front-line was defended by support and reserve units, dispersed on reverse slopes, undulations and in any other cover that could be found, so that they could open machine-gun fire by surprise, from unseen positions and then counter-attack swiftly, before French and British infantry could consolidate captured ground.

The largest German counter-attacks of the Somme battle took place from September 20th – 23rd.,1916, from the Somme north to St Pierre Vaast Wood and were destroyed by French artillery fire. Rather than pack troops into the front-line, local, corps and army reserves were held back, in lines about 2,000 yd. apart, able to make progressively stronger counter-attacks.

Trenches were still dug but were no longer intended to be fought from, being used for shelter during quiet periods, for the movement of reinforcements and supplies and as rallying points and decoys.

Before an attack, the garrison tried to move forwards into shell-holes, to avoid Allied artillery-fire and to surprise attacking infantry with machine-gun fire. Opposite the French, the Germans dug new defences on a reverse slope from the Tortille stream at Allaines to the west end of St Pierre Vaast Wood and from there to Morval, connected to a new fourth position.


## Ancre Heights (Capture of Regina Trench) - 1st October – 11th of November, 1916.

The **Capture of Regina Trench** was one incident during the Battle of the Somme. Regina Trench was the Canadian name for a German trench dug along the north-facing slope of a ridge running from north-west of the village of Le Sars, south-westwards to Stuff Redoubt close to the German fortifications at Thiepval. It was the longest such German trench on the Western Front front during the First World War and very important to the Allies.

It was attacked several times by the Canadian Corps during the Battle of the Ancre Heights and the 5th Canadian Brigade of the 2nd Canadian Division briefly controlled a section of the trench on October 1st., but was repulsed by counter-attacks of the German Marine Brigade (equivalent to an army division), which had been brought from the Belgian coast.

On October 8th., attacks by the 1st Canadian Division and the 3rd Canadian Division on Regina Trench also failed.

On October 21st., the 4th Canadian Division attacked the western portion of Regina Trench, as the 18th (Eastern) Division, 25th

Division and the 39th Division of II Corps, attacked the part further west (known as Stuff Trench to the British).

The Canadians met little opposition gaining the objective, while the II Corps divisions captured Stuff Trench, giving the British control of Thiepval Ridge. Three counter-attacks were repulsed by the Canadians and by October 22nd., more than a thousand Germans had been taken prisoner.

The east end of the trench was captured by the 4th Canadian Division during the night of November 10th. and 11th., 1916.

### The Ancre (Capture of Beaumont Hamel) - 15th. – 18th. of November, 1916.

Close to the village of Beaumont-Hamel, about 800 troops of the First Newfoundland Regiment gathered on July1st., in a support trench they had nicknamed St. John's Road. They were part of a third wave of troops to attack German lines early that morning. The Newfoundlanders began their assault, crossing no man's land in rehearsed lines. Out in the open, they saw that the first waves of British attackers had failed with the troops lying dead, or trapped in no man's land, cut down by machine guns and artillery fire while trying to navigate through the barbed wire.

The Newfoundlanders pressed forward into this firestorm. Some were hit before they even reached the front of the existing British lines. Others died upon reaching the base of the Danger Tree, a prominent tree halfway between the British and German lines, where enemy bullets soon found them.

Less than 30 minutes after leaving their trench, it was all over for the Newfoundlanders. Small groups of survivors attempted in vain to fight on.

Hundreds of injured men were left to fend for themselves on the battlefield through the night, where they died of their wounds or were killed by German snipers.

**More than 700 soldiers of the First Newfoundland Regiment were cut down at Beaumont-Hamel. Of the regiment's 801 members, only 68 could answer roll call by the end of the opening day.**

While Canadians celebrate Memorial day on July 1st., People of Newfoundland and Labrador gather to observe Memorial day and to pay tribute to the valiant men that fought and died defending Beaumont-Hamel.

The battlefield is now a park with a statue of a Caribou, the official emblem of the Newfoundland Regiment on its highest part looking out over the area where so many valiantly died.

### Battle of Vimy Ridge, - 9th. – 14th of April, 1917

The Battle of Vimy Ridge defined Canada as an effective ally and fighting force whose troops knew no retreat. The capture of Vimy Ridge was a magnificent success but at a cost of over 10,000 troops killed and wounded.

The Canadian troops were ordered to seize Vimy Ridge in April 1917. It was a heavily-fortified ridge with a view of seven kilometers of the Allied lines.
The Canadians would be attacking over open graveyard where French attacks had failed with over 100,000 casualties.

The Canadians planned and rehearsed their attack. The infantry were given specialist roles as machine-gunners, rifle-men and grenade-throwers, after weeks of training using models to represent the battlefield, and new maps from aerial photographs. To bring men forward safely for the assault, engineers dug deep tunnels from the rear to the front.

Military mining had long been a feature of war on Vimy Ridge. German, French and British engineers had dug many long tunnels under No Man's Land. They filled them with explosive charges, which blew up enemy trenches, leaving huge craters as new features of the landscape. Working at night, tunnelling companies used the existing tunnels to build a new underground network for the Vimy assault. As well, they dug 12 deep subways, totalling more than five kilometres in length, through which assault troops could move to their jumping-off points. The subways protected them from shelling and permitted the wounded to be brought back from the battlefield. Some subways were quite short, while one, the Goodman Subway, opposite La Folie Farm, was 1.2 kilometres long. All had piped water and most were lit by electricity provided by generators. They also housed telephone lines.

Into the walls of the subways were cut chambers for brigade and battalion headquarters, ammunition stores, communications centres and dressing stations.

The largest of several deep caverns, the Zivy Cave could hold a whole battalion.

Smaller tunnels leading off the subways to the front line—saps they were called (the title, sapper, meaning military engineer or engineer private, derives from this term)—were sealed until Zero Hour and then blown out. At that point, the Canadians would push out to attack, right onto the battlefield.

The maze of tunnels and caverns was one of the most remarkable engineering feats of the war. The extensive underground network would reduce casualties amongst the advancing infantry and returning wounded, and enable supplies to be brought up under less hazardous conditions.

Canadian and British engineers repaired 40 kilometres of road in the Corps' forward area and added 4.8 kilometres of new plank road. They also reconditioned 32 kilometres of tramways, over which light trains, hauled by gasoline engines or mules, carried stores and ammunition.

111

Despite this training and preparation, the key to victory would be an initial strong artillery barrage to isolate enemy trenches and provide a moving wall of high explosives and shrapnel to force the Germans to stay in their deep dugouts and away from their machine-guns.

In the week before the battle, Canadian and British artillery pounded the enemy positions on the ridge, killing many of the German defenders.

A nearly limitless supply of artillery shells and the new 106 fuse, which allowed shells to explode on contact, as opposed to burying themselves in ground, helped to destroy the defenses and barbed wire. The Canadian infantry would be well supported with over 1,000 artillery supporting them.

The four Canadian divisions attacked together and stormed the ridge at 5:30am on April 9th., 1917. More than 15,000 Canadian infantry

*Major Roderick Douglas Graham*
*Red Feather Batallion - Wounded at Vimy*

overran the Germans all along the front. The incredible Canadian bravery and discipline allowed the infantry to move forward under heavy fire, even when their officers were killed. There were countless acts of sacrifice, as Canadians single-handedly charged machine-gun nests or forced the surrender of Germans in protective dugouts.

Hill 145, the highest and most important feature of the Ridge, and where the Vimy monument now stands, was captured in a frontal bayonet charge against machine-gun positions.

Three days of battle delivered final victory. The Canadian operation was an important success, even if the larger British and French offensive, of which it had been a part, had failed.

But it was victory at a heavy cost: 3,598 Canadians were killed and another 7,000 wounded.

The capture of Vimy was more than just an important battlefield victory. For the first time all four Canadian divisions attacked together with men from all regions of Canada present at the battle.

Vimy became a symbol for the sacrifice of the Canadian people. In 1922, the French government ceded to Canada in perpetuity Vimy Ridge, and the land surrounding it. The white marble and sculptures of the Vimy Memorial, unveiled in 1936, stand as a terrible reminder of the 11,285 Canadian soldiers killed in France who have no known graves.

**On A Personal note:**
**Major Roderick Douglas Graham** was my uncle and was wounded at Vimy on April 9th., 1917 and awarded the Military Cross. His comrades in arms described him as follows: *"Another officer who displayed unusual sang froid and heroism after falling wounded during the "Coup of the Red Feather Brigade at Vimy Ridge on Easter Monday, April 9th., 1917" was Lieut. R. Douglas Graham. While leading his platoon in the attack, he was seriously shot by a bullet through the thigh and fell face forward into a shell hole. Consciousness did not forsake him; and as he lay in the shell hole, he repeatedly encouraged his men as they passed by him, exclaiming "Your doing fine boys, your doing fine. Fight them to the finish."* The traditional fighting spirit of his race, the ancient Gaels, and descendant of Dundee was notably displayed.

I was fortunate to have enjoyed his company as a teen ager.

**Major Alistair Fraser,** also my 1st cousin, was wounded at Vimy, and wounded a second time also received the Military Cross. Alistair was Aide d'Camp to General Currie for several years.

He was also Lt. Governor of Nova Scotia in 1954. I remember him visiting my dad in 1954 at South Bar. They shared good whisky and eventually sang Danny Boy.

The Nova Scotia Limousine with the N.S. flag on the front while the chauffer waited outside. I do believe they sent him appropriate refreshments and food while he waited.

## Attach on la Coulotte - 23rd. of April, 1917

The attack on la Coulotte was an additional action by the 2nd. and 3rd Canadian Divisions during the battle of the Scarpe and was mainly a British engagement. It was eventually captured by the Canadian troops in June.

## The Battle of Arleux (28-29 April 1917

This battle was fought to remove the German threat from the southeast flank of Vimy Ridge through a combined British-Canadian attack on the villages of Arleux-en-Gohelle and Gavrelle, which lay 4.7 km to the south of Arleux.

It was successful, but did not lead to any major breakthrough in the German lines.

## The 3rd Battle of the Scarpe (3-4 May 1917)

The 2nd Canadian Battalion, 1st Brigade of 1st Division Canadian Corps, captured Fresnoy-en-Gohelle, 1.8 km east of Arleux, but with over four hundred casualties.

Fresnoy was lost a few days later in this failed offensive, which may explain why the **3rd Battle of the Scarpe** is not better known. For a few details on the 3rd Battle of the Scarpe and Fresnoy,

## Affairs south of Souchez River (3-25 June 1917)

The 3rd and 4th Canadian Divisions were involved in moving the line from Souchez eastward about 5 km to Avion, which was on the outskirts of Lens-Liévin. The action involved the use of gas by the Allied side.

## Capture of Avion (26-29 June 1917)

The 3rd and 4th Canadian Divisions captured **Avion,** just outside of Lens-Liévin, which helped to straighten out the Allied lines and consolidate the earlier gains at Vimy Ridge.

## The Ypres Offensive 1917 (31 July- 18 November 1917) (Also known as the 3rd Battle of Ypres or Battle of Passchendaele)

British, Australian, and New Zealand soldiers fought in these battles during the first three months of the Offensive with 100,000 casualties and little to show for it. This offensive had commenced on July 1 as a diversionary tactic to draw the German forces north and reduce the pressure on the beleaguered French forces further to the south.

## 2nd Battle of Passchendaele (26 October-10 November 1917)

The Canadian Corps' involvement in the Ypres Offensive was at the 2nd Battle of Passchendaele. 20,000 Canadians were involved in this worst of all battles, and over 15,000 of them were casualties.

In four attacks between October 26 and November 10, they managed to take the village of Passchendaele and the high ground overlooking Ypres.

The Battle of Passchendaele was probably the worst engagement of the entire war in terms of lives lost and injuries.

## Battle of Cambrai (20 Nov-3 Dec 1917)

The Battle of Cambrai was fought in the region between **Arras and Cambrai** to the southeast. The Canadian Cavalry Brigade and the Newfoundland Regiment fought with distinction in this British-led battle, which involved the first successful use of tanks, and the Newfoundland Regiment was granted the title "Royal" - the only regiment so honoured during the war.

## The Battle of Amiens "Black Day of the German Army" (8-11 August 1918)

In a surprise attack from trenches east of Amiens, Canadian and Australian troops, along with 600 tanks, broke through German defences and moved about 12 km the first day. French troops to the south and British to the north also advanced and German soldiers began to surrender by the thousands, a clear indication that morale was faltering in the German army.

It was the beginning of the end, although it would still be nearly three months before the war was over. In the meantime, German soldiers were surrendering in large numbers.

On October 26, with the Australians and New Zealanders on their right and the British on their left, the Canadian Corps became engaged in the **Battle of Passchendaele**. In four attacks between October 26 and November 10, they managed to take the village of Passchendaele and the high ground overlooking Ypres.

**The Ypres Offensive** resulted in 260,000 casualties, which included over 15,000 Canadian dead and wounded during the Battle of Passchendaele, which was perhaps the most horrific engagement of the entire war.

## Action around Damery (15-17 August 1918)

All four Canadian Divisions were involved in the action around Damery, which was about 39 km southeast of Amiens.

## The Arras Offensive or 2nd Battle of Arras (26 August-3 September 1918)

This offensive was an allied offensive spearheaded by the Canadian Corps which pushed eastward from Arras in two major engagements, one called the **Battle of the Scarpe**, after the Scarpe River, and the other the Battle of **Drocourt-Quéant,** named after the towns at either end of a strong German trench system that the allied forces were determined to capture.

### The 4th Battle of the Scarpe (26-30 August 1918)

In this battle, the allied forces, including the 2nd and 3rd Divisions of the Canadian Corps, moved about 8 km eastward from Arras capturing Monchy-le-Preux and the villages of Guemappe and Wancourt along a line between the Scarpe River on the north and Neuville-Vitasse on the south.

It brought them to the heavily defended German line of **Drocourt-Quéant**, which was the next objective.

### Battle of the Drocourt-Quéant Line (2-3 September 1918)

The 1st and 4th Divisions of the Canadian Corps took the lead in this battle, which moved the allied forces eastward another 8 km with the capture of Dury and the collapse of the Drocourt-Quéant Line. The Allies now moved forward to prepare to take the next obstacle, the **Canal Du Nord.**

### Battle of the Canal du Nord (27 September-3 October 1918)

The 1st and 4th Canadian Divisions, with reinforcements from the 3rd, pushed across Canal-du-Nord on September 27 and captured the village of Bourlon, which was about 14 km southeast of Dury and 12 km west of Cambrai, the major German supply centre for the region.

On the following day, they captured Raillencourt-Sainte-Olle and Sailly-lez-Cambrai about 5 km directly west of Cambrai.

On the 29th, they captured Sancourt and held Blécourt briefly about 7 km north of Cambrai with two battalions fighting to the edge of Neuville-Saint-Rémy, a suburb of Cambrai. Nearby Tilloy-les-

Cambrai fell to the PPCLI on September 30 and the position was consolidated the following day.

The exhausted 1st and 4th Divisions now went into reserve and were replaced by the 2nd and 3rd Canadian Divisions on the front lines.

## Battle of Cambrai (8-9 October 1818)

On October 9, the 3rd Canadian Division captured Cambrai and joined the 24th British Division that had come up from the south.

## Battle of Le Cateau (9 October 1918)

The Canadian Cavalry Brigade with the British 4th Army advanced nearly 13 km, captured weapons and over 400 prisoners as well as disrupted German demolition efforts.

## Pursuit to the Selle (9-12 October 1918)

On October 9, the 2nd Canadian Division captured the towns of Ramillies, Escaudoeuvres, and Eswars northeast of Cambrai. On October 10, it took the villages of Thun-Saint-Martin and Naves, 2-3 km further east. By October 12, the frontlines of the Canadian Corps stretched along a 12 km stretch northeast of Cambrai, from Aubencheul-au-Bac on the northwest to Iwuy on the southeast.

## Battle of Valenciennes (2 November 1918)

During October, the Canadian Corps steadily moved east until they reached Valenciennes on November 1. Because there were so many French refugees in the city, the Canadians did not press the offensive on Valenciennes directly. However, even though the Germans held out here and at nearby Marly, over 800 of their soldiers were killed and 1800 more captured by the Canadians on November 2nd.

On the same day, the 4th Canadian Division captured the village of Saint-Saulvé about 1.5 km east of Valenciennes and by November 4, the 3rd and 4th Canadian Divisions had reached Vicq and Onnaing about 7-8 km further east. They were now about 25 km from Mons.

## Passage of the Grande Honelle (5-7 November 1918)

The 3rd and 4th Canadian Divisions captured Vicq and Quarouble on November 5 and were in control of the Petite and Grande Honelle Rivers by November 6. On November 7, the 3rd Canadian Division had crossed the border into Belgium and taken control of Hensies.

To the south, the 2nd Canadian Division took Élouges, and were still moving east. They were now less than 15 km from Mons.

## Capture of Mons (8-11 November 1918)

On November 8, the **3rd Canadian Division** captured Thivencelle and Saint-Aybert to the west of Hensies, then moved east again. On November 9, the **Princess Patricia's Canadian Light Infantry, 3rd Canadian Division**, moved 8 km east to Jemappes, which was less than 5 km west of Mons. The **2nd Canadian Division** to the south reached Dour on November 8 and Bougnies, about 7 km south of Jemappes, the following day.

On November 10, the **2nd Canadian Division** reached the village of Hyon on the outskirts of Mons and by 11 p.m. platoons were moving into the city.

Early the following morning, they were in control of Mons. The war ended where it had started on August 23rd., 1914, but with a better result.

It was another great Canadian success.

# CHAPTER 8

# NO MAN'S LAND

No Man's Land was the piece of land separating the warring parties. The term goes back as far as William the Conqueror. It was not a pretty sight with shell holes filled with water, unexploded shells and often bodies from either side. Often the areas were littered with abandoned war machinery and the risk of snipers. Generally a lot of barbed wire was used by both sides along areas where an attack could be expected. Often there were multiple rows of barbed wire.

The shell holes often became bogs with barbed wire below the surface. If a soldier got tangled in barbed wire and was not rescued he would eventually bleed to death.

When the troops decided to stay in the shell hole or trench, sentries would be appointed and tasks would be undertaken such as digging latrines, fortifying the area with sand bags, barbed wire and building fire-steps to give the soldier a better view when firing on the enemy. Listening posts would be established outside the trench to give some advanced warning of the enemy approaching.

The soldiers on both sides would be dirty, unshaved and often covered with vermin, and in this condition for days if not weeks. Soldiers would often wish to be wounded enough to be taken out of service but also knew that  because of the lack of stretcher bearers they could be left behind.

The enemy would use flares to light up the no man's land area and sentries would not move and give up their position, even at the risk of being hit with a flare.

The width of no man's land, or you could say, the distance separating the opposing sides, could be anywhere from 8 yards to 500 yards and the area filled with shell holes of unknown depth. There are stories of soldiers in water to their waste in shell holes fighting for up to 40 hours. Soldiers would often take control of a shell hole as it got them closer to the enemy, gave them some protection and helped them to get information on the enemy position. From shell hole positions, soldiers could crawl forward at night to get closer to the enemy and perhaps capture other soldiers. They would have camouflage made of the surrounding plants and wreaths on their helmets. This was the most dangerous of the wartime tasks and soldiers had their faces blackened and their rifle, bayonet and revolver with no unnecessary items.

The British night patrols were common and the Germans used flares hanging from small parachutes to light up the positions of the advancing enemy soldiers on no man's land and kill or capture them. The darker the night the better as their camouflaged bodies moved through the barbed wire zones, stopping periodically and listening perhaps for an hour or more before moving forward. The  other soldiers anxiously wait at the trench for their return.

At some point the patrol might hear faint voices from the German trench but they are also aware that there could be a German night patrol, possibly close to them. Often the bush moving might be an animal so caution is important. At night the imagination can play tricks and the soldier might imagine bushes might be moving towards him.

The job of night patrol was only for the bravest and not the faint of heart.

# CHAPTER 9

# RATES OF PAY

**People generally didn't enlist in the service for the money.**

**Daily Rates:** Wages were low, starting at $1.00 per day. The average wage, at the time, was $2.00 a day and higher. As the ranks increased so did the wages and allowances. The government provided a dependant allowance, or "Separation Allowance", for those leaving a wife or mother behind. In many cases this was not sufficient.

**Specialty Trades:** People such as engineers, miners, sappers and others with specialty skills and working in exceptionally dangerous situations, received a higher rate of pay.

**Patriotic Fund:** This was a charity established to help families in need while the wage earner was overseas. There were no fixed amounts and amounts determined by the need.

**I believe that, at the time the best paying compant was the Ford motor Company at $5.00 per day.**

# Pay Rates During WW 1

| Rank | Basic Daily Pay | Daily Overseas Allowance | Monthly Separation Allowance |
|---|---|---|---|
| Privates, Drivers, Cooks, Buglers, Drummers, Trumpeters | $1.00 | $0.10 | $20.00 |
| 2nd. Corporal, Bombardier | $1.05 | $0.10 | $20.00 |
| Corporal | $1.10 | $0.10 | $20.00 |
| Sergeant | $1.35 | $0.15 | $25.00 |
| Quartermaster Sgt, Orderly Room Clerk | $1.50 | $0.20 | $25.00 |
| Staff, Color Sergeant, Sergeant Major | $1.60 | $0.20 | $25.00 |
| Quartermaster Sergeant | $1.80 | $0.20 | $25.00 |
| Warrant Officer | $2.00 | $0.30 | $30.00 |
| Lieutenant | $2.00 | $0.60 | $30.00 |
| Quartermaster, Paymaster, Captain | $3.00 | $0.75 | $40.00 |
| Major | $4.00 | $1.00 | $50.00 |
| Lieutenant Colonel | $5.00 | $1.25 | $60.00 |
| Colonel | $6.00 | $1.50 | $60.00 |
| Brigade Major | $6.00 | $3.00 | $60.00 |
| Brigade Commander | $9.00 | $3.00 | $60.00 |
| ADC to Commander | $3.00 | $3.00 | $40.00 |
| Div. Paymaster, Gen Staff Officer 3rd Grade | $5.00 | $3.00 | $60.00 |
| Chief Paymaster, Ass. Dir. Medical Services, Gen. Staff Officer, 2nd. Grade | $8.00 | $3.00 | $60.00 |
| General Staff Officer, 1st. Grade | $10.00 | $3.00 | $60.00 |
| Major General | $20.00 | $4.00 | $60.00 |

# CHAPTER 10

# PIP – SQUEAK - WILFRED

These three medals would be awarded to those who enlisted in WW1.

The **Mons Star** was only awarded to those who enlisted between August 5th., 1914 and October 5th., 1915. 2,350,000 were awarded.

The **Silver war medal** recorded the end of the war and was received by anyone serving between 1914 and 1920. There were 6,000,500 struck in silver and 110,000 in bronze and awarded to Maltese, Chinese, Egyptian, Indian and other labour corps.

The **Victory medal** was awarded to all who received the star medal and many who received the British War Medal. Those receiving these medals had their name, rank and service number impressed on the edge of the medal.

The medals were nicknamed: Pip, Squeak and Wilfred after a popular British comic strip. Pip was a dog, Squeak was a penguin and Wilfred a baby rabbit.

**Question:** Is it legal to wear medals other than those earned by the wearer?

**Answer:** In Britain and Australia and some other countries it is legal, however in Canada it is a criminal offense to wear medals the wearer has not earned. That being said; those medals are only worn on the right side.

Looking at pages in the Legion and other magazines will find the majority of people with medals on their right side. In most cases they are medals of family members and they display them with pride and respect.

On November 1st., 2020 a person called the RCL branch 582 registering a complaint that there was an old veteran wearing WW1 medals that were not his. As my wife and I were the only ones there selling Poppies, I was indeed the culprit. Was it a crime? Yes it was. Could I be charged? Yes I could.

I was born when my father was 59 years old so I missed a generation. **The medals were earned by five of my 1st cousins and one uncle who served in WW1.** One cousin and an uncle were alive when I was in my early teens in the mid 50's.

**Nursing Sister Marjorie Fraser** who drowned when the Hospital ship Llandovery Castle was torpedoed on June 28th., 1918.

**Nursing Sister Harriet Graham** (Marjorie's cousin) who, With Marjorie helped set up the first Canadian hospital in France.

**Lt. Gibson Laurier Fraser** (Marjorie's brother) Killed in action in March, 1918.

**Lt. Wendell Stuart Graham** (Harriet Graham's brother) served in France.

**Major Allister Fraser,** (Marjorie's other brother) Wounded at Vimy Ridge and wounded again, Received the Military Cross and was also Aide d'Camp to General Currie.

**Major Roderick Graham** of the Red Feather Battalion (my Uncle) Wounded at Vimy and received the Military Cross. I read his comrades writing where he was lying in the mud at Vimy Ridge with a bullet in his hip urging his men on.

Will I continue to wear these medals? Most certainly I will. I will wear them with the greatest of **Humility, Pride, Love,**

**Respect and Admiration** and hope others will remember those who gave so much for our freedom.

- **THE MONS STAR** is particularly important to Canadians. The battle of Mons, Belgium was fought and lost on August 23rd,1914, by the British to slow the German invasion of France.

- On November 10th., 1918, three Canadian regiments freed Mons and the hundreds of French occupants.

# I WILL REMEMBER THEM

# CHAPTER 11

# ARMISTICE

## Armistice and End of the War (11 November 1918)

At 6:30 a.m. the headquarters of the Canadian Corps received word that an armistice had been signed and the war would come to an end at 11:00 a.m. After nearly five years of hell, the soldiers could finally put down their guns. the incessant boom of artillery abruptly went silent along the Western Front in France.

It took hours for the reality to sink in. World War I, the bloodiest conflict in human history, with more than 37 million casualties had finally ended.

But the war ended with an armistice, an agreement in which both sides agree to stop fighting, rather than a surrender. For both sides, an armistice was the fastest way to end the war.

By November 1918, both sides had been fighting each other for four years were pretty much out of gas. German offensives that year had heavy casualties, and in late summer and fall, the British, French and U.S. forces had pushed them steadily back.

With the United States able to send more and more fresh troops into combat, the Germans were outmatched. As Germany's allies crumbled around them as well, the war's outcome seemed clear.

Both sides were ready for the killing and destruction to stop. Berlin is a long way from France. There was a need to end the war as soon as possible as long as the Allies could achieve peace with victory."

Germany asked to negotiate an armistice. In fact, the Germans had started talking about an armistice in early October. At first they tried to go through U.S. President Woodrow Wilson, fearing that the British and the French would insist upon harsh terms. But that end run didn't succeed. The Germans finally sent a radio message to Marshal Ferdinand Foch, commander-in-chief of the Allied forces, requesting permission to send a delegation through the lines to negotiate an armistice, and asked for a general cease-fire. He ignored the cease-fire request, but gave the Germans permission to come.

At 8:00 p.m. on November 7, three automobiles carefully made their way through the nightmarish landscape of artillery craters and barbed wire in no-man's land in northern France, as a German bugler sounded a truce and another soldier waved a white flag. The German envoys switched to a French car and then boarded a train, and traveled through the night. On the morning of November 8, they pulled into a railroad siding in the Forest of Compiègne, alongside Foch's railroad car. That was where the meeting would take place.

There wasn't much of a negotiation. When the Germans asked if he had an Allied offer, Foch responded, "I have no proposals to make." His instructions from the Allied governments were to simply present an as-is deal. French General Maxime Weygand then read the terms that the Allies had decided upon to the Germans.

According to Lowry's account, the Germans became distraught when they heard that they would have to disarm, fearing that they'd be unable to defend their teetering government against communist revolutionaries. But they had little leverage. In the early morning hours of November 11, Erzberger and Foch met for the final negotiations. According to Lowry, the German emissary tried his best to persuade Foch to make the agreement less severe. Foch made a few small changes, including letting the Germans keep a few of their weapons. Finally, just before dawn, the agreement was signed.

The Germans agreed to pull their troops out of France, Belgium and Luxembourg within 15 days, or risk becoming prisoners of the Allies.

They had to turn over their arsenal, including 5,000 artillery pieces, 25,000 machine guns and 1,700 airplanes, along with 5,000 railroad locomotives, 5,000 trucks and 150,000 wagons. Germany also had to give up the contested territory of Alsace-Lorraine.

And they agreed to Allied forces occupying German territory along the Rhine, where they would stay until 1930.

"The Allies wouldn't have given Germany better terms because they felt that they had to defeat Germany and Germany could not be allowed to get away with it," Cuthbertson said. "There's also a sense that an armistice has to ensure that the enemy are not strong enough to start the war again anytime soon."

After the celebrations on both sides of the Atlantic had died down, two months later a conference was convened at Versailles, just outside Paris, to work out a final peace treaty. But the Allied powers all had different agendas.

It wasn't until May that the Allies agreed to a common position that they could present to the Germans.

In the agreement that was signed in June, vanquished Germany was forced to accept harsh terms, including paying reparations that eventually amounted to $37 billion (nearly $492 billion in today's dollars). That humiliation and the lasting bitterness it engendered helped pave the way to another World War two decades later.

November 11th., itself would become a hallowed day. In 1919, President Wilson proclaimed the first Armistice Day, The day is also now known as Remembrance Day in the Commonwealth of Nations. And in 1954, the U.S. Congress changed its name to Veterans Day to honour service members who had served in World War II and the Korean War as well.

# CHAPTER 12

## Kimmel Park Mutiny – 4th. – 5th., of March, 1919

Still in England in March, Canadian troops were incensed that ships seemed to be available for American forces, most of whom were comparative newcomers to the war, unlike the Canadians. Rumours also persisted of discrimination in the employment market in favour of officers and there was news of lay-offs and wage cuts, in response to a recession caused by the great war debt. Soldiers realized that the longer they were delayed in England the more difficult time they would have securing employment in a dwindling job market. By late February unemployment in Canada rose sharply as well shipping delays. These factors combined to create an environment conducive to mutiny.

The mutineers were Canadian soldiers who had fought well for Britain, stuck in the mud of North Wales, waiting impatiently to get back to Canada – four months after the end of the war. The 15,000 Canadian troops that concentrated at Kinmel didn't know about the strikes that had held up the fuelling of ships and which had caused food shortages.

The men were on half rations, there was no coal for the stove in the cold grey huts, and they hadn't been paid for over a month.

Forty-two had to sleep in a hut meant for thirty, so they each took turns sleeping on the floor, with one blanket each. In all, between November 1918 and June 1919, there were thirteen instances of riots or disturbances involving Canadian troops in England.

The most serious of these occurred at Kimmel Park on 4 and 5 March 1919, when dissatisfaction over delays in sailing resulted in five men being killed and 23 wounded. Seventy eight men were arrested, of whom 25 were convicted of mutiny and given sentences varying from 90 days' detention to ten years' penal servitude.

Redeployment was sped up and by 25 March approximately 15,000 soldiers had departed Kimmel Camp. Contemporary sources confirm that Canadian authorities expedited sailings for the soldiers of Kinmel Park Camp and immediately after the riot the SS Adriatic and the SS Celtic were reallocated to the troops of Kimmel providing berths for approximately 5000 soldiers.

It was a sad situation that those who fought so hard, had given so much, were treated so badly.   Has anything really changed?

# CHAPTER 13

## End of war/Treaty of Versailles – 28<sup>th</sup> of June 1919.

The Treaty of Versailles, signed in June 1919 at the Palace of Versailles in Paris at the end of World War I, codified peace terms between the victorious Allies and Germany.

The Treaty of Versailles held Germany responsible for starting the war and imposed harsh penalties in terms of loss of territory, massive reparations payments and demilitarization.

Far from the "peace without victory" that U.S. President Woodrow Wilson had outlined in his famous Fourteen Points in early 1918, the Treaty of Versailles humiliated Germany while failing to resolve the underlying issues that had led to war in the first place.

Economic distress and resentment of the treaty within Germany helped fuel the ultra-nationalist sentiment that led to the rise of Adolf Hitler and his Nazi Party, as well as the coming of a World War II just two decades later.

The Fourteen Points

In a speech to Congress in January 1918, Wilson laid out his idealistic vision for the post-war world. In addition to specific territorial settlements based on an Entente victory, Wilson's so-called Fourteen Points emphasized the need for national self-determination for Europe's different ethnic populations.

Wilson also proposed the founding of a "general association of nations" that would mediate international disputes and foster cooperation between different nations in the hopes of preventing war on such a large scale in the future. This organization eventually became known as the League of Nations.

## Wilson's Fourteen Points are summarized below:

1. Diplomacy should be public, with no secret treaties.
2. All nations should enjoy free navigation of the seas.
3. Free trade should exist among all nations, putting an end to economic barriers between countries.
4. All countries should reduce arms in the name of public safety.
5. Fair and impartial rulings in colonial claims.
6. Restore Russian territories and freedom.
7. Belgium should be restored to independence.
8. Alsace-Lorraine should be returned to France and France should be fully liberated.
9. Italy's frontiers should be drawn along clearly recognizable lines of nationality.
10. People living in Austria-Hungary should be granted self-determination.
11. The Balkan states should also be guaranteed self-determination and independence.
12. Turks and those under Turkish rule should be granted self-determination.
13. An independent Poland should be created.
14. A general association of nations must be formed to mediate international disputes.

When German leaders signed the armistice ending hostilities in World War I on November 11, 1918, they believed this vision articulated by Wilson would form the basis for any future peace treaty. This would not prove to be the case.

## The Paris Peace Conference opened on January 18, 1919.

The Terms of the Versailles Treaty.

The "Big Four" leaders of the victorious Western nations—**Wilson** of the United States, **David Lloyd George** of Great Britain, **Georges Clemenceau** of France and, to a lesser extent,

**Vittorio Orlando of Italy**—dominated the peace negotiations in Paris. Germany and the other defeated powers, Austria-Hungary, Bulgaria and Turkey, were not represented at the conference; nor was Russia, which had fought as one of the Allied powers until 1917, when the country's new Bolshevik government concluded a separate peace with Germany and withdrew from the conflict.

The Big Four themselves had competing objectives in Paris:

a) Clemenceau's main goal was to protect France from yet another attack by Germany. He sought heavy reparations from Germany as a way of limiting German economic recovery after the war and minimizing this possibility.

b) Lloyd George, on the other hand, saw the rebuilding of Germany as a priority in order to re-establish the nation as a strong trading partner for Great Britain.

c) For his part, Orlando wanted to expand Italy's influence and shape it into a major power that could hold its own alongside the other great nations.

d) Wilson opposed Italian territorial demands, as well as previously existing arrangements regarding territory between the other Allies; instead, he wanted to create a new world order along the lines of the Fourteen Points. The other leaders saw Wilson as too naive and idealistic, and his principles were difficult to translate into policy.

In the end, the European Allies imposed harsh peace terms on Germany, forcing the nation to surrender around 10 percent of its territory and all of its overseas possessions.

Other key provisions of the Treaty of Versailles called for the demilitarization and occupation of the Rhineland, limited Germany's army and navy, forbade it to maintain an air force, and required it to conduct war crimes trials against Kaiser Wilhelm II and other leaders for their aggression.

Most importantly, Article 231 of the treaty, better known as the "war guilt clause," forced Germany to accept full responsibility for starting World War I and pay enormous reparations for Allied war losses.

The Treaty of Versailles was signed on June 28, 1919, exactly five years after the Serbian nationalist Gavrilo Princip assassinated Archduke Franz Ferdinand and his wife in Sarajevo, sparking the outbreak of the war.

Though the treaty included a covenant creating the League of Nations, an international organization aimed at preserving peace, the harsh terms imposed on Germany helped ensure that peace would not last for long.

Germans were furious about the treaty, seeing it as a dictated peace; they resented the sole blame of war being placed at them.

Upon ratification of the Treaty of Versailles the Central Powers (Germany, Austria-Hungary, Turkey and Bulgaria), as the defeated powers, were required to give war reparations in either cash or material to the Allied Powers. Payment would be in cash or in kind (material).

Turkey, Austria and Hungary were in a poor financial position and were exempted from this. Bulgaria paid part of the requirement and the balance was cancelled.

The German payment requirement was to be enforced and started in 1921 with $32 billion US dollars.

In 1923, France occupied the Ruhr to enforce payment. This naturally caused an international incident resulting in a revised payment plan. Payment plans were again revised in 1928 that would see payments completed by 1988.

With the collapse of the German economy in 1931 payments were suspended for a year and cancelled. The total amount that Germany paid was less than $6,000,000 US dollars by 1932.

The final payments of the remaining balance were paid on October 3rd., 2010

The **Prime Minister of France, Georges Clemenceau,** was determined that any just peace required Germany to pay reparations for the damages it caused. He considered reparations as a way to weaken Germany to ensure it could never threaten France again. His position was shared by the French citizens.

**British Prime Minister David Lloyd George** opposed these proposed overbearing reparations, suggesting a lesser sum, which would be less harmful in the long term to the German economy as he wanted Germany as a trading partner.

**Wilson** opposed these positions wanting no indemnity should be imposed upon Germany.

Keynes was only one prominent critic of the Treaty of Versailles. The French military leader **Ferdinand Foch** refused to attend the signing ceremony, as he thought the treaty didn't do enough to secure against a future German threat, while the U.S. Congress failed to ratify the treaty, and later concluded a separate peace with Germany; the United States would never join the League of Nations.

In the years following the Treaty of Versailles, many ordinary Germans believed they had been betrayed by those leaders who signed the treaty and formed the post-war government. Radical right-wing political forces—especially the National Socialist Workers' Party, or the Nazis—would gain support in the 1920s and '30s by promising to reverse the humiliation of the Versailles Treaty.

With the onset of the Great Depression after 1929, economic unrest destabilized the already vulnerable Weimar government, setting the stage for Nazi leader Adolf Hitler's fateful rise to power in 1933.

# CHAPTER 14

# MINING

When we picture soldiers fighting we visualize marching soldiers or soldiers driving tanks. While this is an integral part of the fighting, a substantial amount of work in done with underground tunnelling by Tunnelling companies numbering hundreds of tunnelers (Sappers) and engineers.

These tunnelling warfare units did offensive and defensive mining involving placing and maintaining mines under enemy lines.

Some of the work in this area was done by the New Zealand Tunnelling Company.

The New Zealand Tunnelling Company was a tu          f the Royal New Zealand Electrical and Mechanica

Initially, the miners, or moles as they were often referred to use a method called "Clay Kicking". This worked fine in small diameter tunnels where the tunnelers sat and were supported by a backrest with their feet towards the face.

Using a small spade they tossed the earth or rock one of their mates who would move it to the rea sure this was a toy compared to the Pan shovels they used to earn their livings.

They also constructed deep underground dugouts to accommodate troops often equipping these underground dugouts with electricity, gas proof doors, telephone exchanges and running water.

In one tunnel, a hospital, tram line and 750 circuit telephone system was built. In some cases they were actually undetected behind enemy lines.

A Canadian tunnelling unit was formed from men on the battlefield, plus three other tunnelling Battalions consisting of miners from Canada and most from Nova Scotia and the Cape Breton Mining areas.

That I will deal with under a separate cover called;

# "The Cape Breton Miners and WW 1" It will pay tribute to the many miners who lost their lives in defense of King and Country.

## "We Will Remember them"

## Many of the Miners from the 1st and 2nd Tunneling Companies and from some engineering Batallions

| Lieutenant | Spencer, Roy Aubrey | Glace Bay, C.B., N.S. |
|---|---|---|
| Lieutenant | George Morley | Glace Bay, CB., N.S. |
| 501144 Trooper | Cameron, Daniel F. | Dominion, C.B., N.S. |
| 501143 Trooper | Butts, Walter | Glace Bay, C.B., N.S. |
| 501232 Trooper | Corbett, Allan | Victoria Mines, C.B., N.S. |
| 501230 Trooper | Daley, James | Sydney Mines, C.B., N.S. |
| 501145 Trooper | John Deacon, Alonze | Dominion, No 3, C.B. |
| 501313 Trooper | Fraser, Thomas | Margaree, C.B. |
| 501311 Trooper | Gillis, Angus | Hawkesbury, C.B., N.S. |
| 501147 Trooper | Gillis, Charles | Glace Bay, C.B., N.S. |
| 501226 Trooper | Gouthro, Joseph Leonard | French Vale, C.B., N.S. |
| 501137 L. Cpl | Hall, Harry | New Aberdeen, C. B., N.S. |
| 501279 Trooper | Hanes, William John | Sutherland's River, N.S. |
| 503258 Private | Leslie, Daniel | Inverness, C.B. |
| 469682 Private | Lynk, Daniel (64th. Battalion | Glace Bay, C.B. |
| 501216 Trooper | McDonald, Alex. Allan | Inverness, C.B. |
| 501222 Trooper | McDonald, Archie Kennedy | Dominion No. 1, C.B. |
| 501221 L. Cpl | McDonald, Rod. Herbert | New Aberdeen, C.B. |
| 501015 Trooper | McDonald, Stanley | River Dennis, C.B. |
| 501234 Trooper | McDonald, Vincent | Georges River, C.B. |
| 501150 Trooper | McDougall, Daniel | Glace Bay, C.B. |
| 501151 Trooper | McKinnon, Daniel | Brick Grove, C.B. |
| 501287 Trooper | McKinnon, William | River Dennis, C.B. |
| 501195 Trooper | McLean, John L. | Sydney Mines, N.S. |

| | | |
|---|---|---|
| 501152 Trooper | McLean Lachlan J. | Dominion No. 1, C.B. |
| 501225 Trooper | McLean, Wilfred Murray | Baddeck, C.B. |
| 501153 Trooper | McMullan, Joseph | Reserve, C.B. |
| 501154 Trooper | McNeil, Michael F. | New Waterford, C.B., N.S |
| 501155 Trooper | McNeil, Peter | Florence, C.B. |
| 501149 Trooper | McNeil, Stephen | North Sydney, C.B. |
| 501233 L.Cpl | Morrison, Hector James | Glace Bay, C.B. |
| 501228 L.Cpl | Murphy, James Reginald | Dominion No. 1, C.B. |
| 501157 Trooper | Petrie, John | Dominion No. 1, C.B. |
| 501227 Trooper | Roberts, John | Glace Bay, C.B. |
| 501159 Trooper | Rogers, Edward | Glace Bay, C.B. |
| 501238 L.Cpl | Slade, Phillip | Dominion No. 6, C.B. |
| 501160 Trooper | Slade, William | Dominion, #6, C.B. |
| 501320 Trooper | Steele, Edward | Glace Bay, C.B. |
| 501239 Trooper | Tutty Joseph | Sydney Mines, C.B. |
| 503439 Private | Way, Harry Charles | Sydney Mines, C.B. |
| | | |

**There are many also from mainland Nov Scotia but we will deal with them under separate title.**

# CHAPTER 15

## ABBREVIATIONS
## GENERAL

A. ...................................................................Branch of Adjutant-General.
A./or a/........................................................Acting.
A.A. ............................................................Army Act. or Anti-Aircraft.
AAA or aaa. ................................................Full stop.
A.A. & Q.M.G. .............................Assistant Adjutant and Quartermaster-General.
A. & P.M.G. ................................................Accountant and Paymaster General.
A.A.G. ........................................................Assistant Adjutant-General.
A.D.C. ........................................................Aide-de-Camp.
Addsd. .......................................................Addressed.
A.D.S. .....................Advanced Dressing Station, or Assistant Director of Signalling.
Adjt. ..........................................................Adjutant.
A.D.M.S.......................................................Assistant Director of Medical Services.
Adv. ...........................................................Advanced.
A.D.V.S. .....................................................Assistant Director of Veterinary Services.
A.G. ...........................................................Adjutant-General.
Amb. ..........................................................Ambulance.
Amm. Col. ..................................................Ammunition Column.
Anzac. ........................................................Australian and New Zealand Army
Corps. A.O. ................................................Army Order.
A.P.M. ........................................................Assistant Provost-Marshal.
A.Q.M.G. ....................................................Assistant Quartermaster-General.
Arty. ..........................................................Artillery.
Bde(s) ........................................................Brigade(s).
B.E.F. ..........................................................British Expeditionary Force.
B.G.G.S. ......................................................Brigadier-General, General Staff.
B.L. .............................................................Breech loading.
B.M. ...........................................................Brigade Major.
Bn(s) ..........................................................Battalion(s).
Br.-Gen. ......................................................Brigadier-General.
Bty. ............................................................Battery.
Cav. ............................................................Cavalry.
C.D.A. ........................................................Canadian Divisional Artillery.
Cdn. Arty. ..................................................Canadian Artillery.
C.C.S. ..........................................................Casualty Clearing Station.
Cdn.Div. .....................................................Canadian Division.
Cdn. Inf. Bde. .............................................Canadian Infantry Brigade.
C.E. .............................................................Canadian Engineers, or Chief Engineer.
C.E.F. ..........................................................Canadian Expeditionary Force.
C.F.A. ..........................................................Canadian Field Artillery.
C.G.A. .........................................................Canadian Garrison Artillery.
C.G.S. ..........................................................Chief of the General Staff.
C.I.A.A. .......................................................Chief Inspector of Arms and Ammunition.
C.I.B. ...........................................................Canadian Infantry Brigade.
C.I.G.S. ........................................................Chief of the Imperial General Staff.
C. in-C. ........................................................Commander-in-Chief.

| | |
|---|---|
| C.M. | Canadian Militia. |
| C.O. | Commanding Officer. |
| Comdg. | Commanding. |
| Comdr. | Commander. |
| C.O.O. | Chief Ordnance Officer. |
| Coy(s) | Company. Companies. |
| C.R.A. | Officer Commanding, Royal Artillery. |
| C.R.E. | Officer Commanding, Royal Engineers. |
| C.S.M. | Company Sergeant-Major. |
| C.T. | Communication trench. |
| D.A. | Divisional Artillery, or Dominion Arsenal. |
| D.A.A.G. | Deputy Assistant Adjutant-General. |
| D.A.A. & Q.M.G. | Deputy Assistant Adjutant and Quartermaster General. |
| D.A.B. | Detachement d'Armee de Belgique. |
| D.A.D.M.S. | Deputy Assistant Director of Medical Services. |
| D.A.D.O.S. | Deputy Assistant Director of Ordnance Services. |
| D.A.G. | Deputy Adjutant-General. |
| D.D.M.S. | Deputy Director of Medical Services. |
| D.D.O.S. | Deputy Director of Ordnance Services. |
| D.D.V.S. | Deputy Director of Veterinary Services. |
| D.E.O.S. | Director of Equipment and Ordnance Services. |
| Det. | Detachment. |
| D.G.M.S. | Director-General of Medical Services. |
| Div. | Division, or Divisional. |
| Div. Amm. Col. | Divisional Ammunition Column. |
| Div. Arty. | Divisional Artillery. |
| D.M. | Deputy Minister. |
| D.M.O. | Director of Military Operations. |
| D.M.S. | Director of Medical Services. |
| D.M.T. | Director of Military Training. |
| D.O.C. | District Officer Commanding. |
| D. of C. | Director of Contracts. |
| D. of S.&T. | Director of Supplies and Transport. |
| d.o.w. | Died of Wounds. |
| E.A. | Enemy Aircraft. |
| Engrs. | Engineers. |
| Fd. Amb. | Field Ambulance. |
| Fd. Arty. Bde. | Field Artillery Brigade. |
| Fd. Coy. | Field Company. |
| F.L.T. | Front t Line Trench. |
| F.O.O. | Forward Observing Officer. |
| F.S.R. | Field Service Regulations. |
| G.H.Q. | British General Headquarters. |
| G.O. | General Order. |
| G.O.C. | General Officer Commanding. |
| G.O.C.-in-C. | General Officer Commanding-in-Chief. |
| G.P.N. | Groupe Provisoire du Nord. |
| G.Q.G. | Grand Quartier General. i.e. French |
| G.H.Q. G. or G.S. | General Staff, or General Service. |
| G.S.O. 1, 2,3 | General Staff Officer, let, 2nd or 3rd |
| Grade. H.A.R. | Heavy Artillery Reserve. |
| H.B. | Heavy Battery. |
| H.E. | High Explosive. |

| | |
|---|---|
| How. | Howitzer. |
| H.Q.(Hd. Qrs.) | Headquarters. |
| H.T. | Horse Transport. |
| H.V. | High velocity. |
| i/e | in charge of, or in command. |
| I.G. | Inspector-General. |
| J.A.G. | Judge Advocate General. |
| k. in a. | Killed in action. |
| K.R. | The King's Regulations for the Army. |
| L.B. | Landwehr Brigade. (German). |
| L.E. | Lee-Enfield. |
| L.I.R. | Landwehr Infantry Regiment. (German). |
| L. of C. | Line, or Lines of Communication. |
| M. & D. | Militia and Defence. |
| M.D. | Military District. |
| M.D.S. | Main Dressing Station. |
| M.G., G.S. | Major-General, General Staff. |
| M.G(s) | Machine gun(s). |
| M.G.O. | Master-General of the Ordnance. |
| Mk. | Mark. |
| M.M.L. | Manual of Military Law. |
| M.O. | Medical Officer, or Militia Order. |
| M.P. | Military Police or Member of Parliament. |
| M.T. | Mechanical Transport. |
| N.C.O. | Non-commissioned Officer. |
| N.D.H.Q. | National Defence Headquarters. |
| N.P. or N.P.A.M. | Non-Permanent Active Militia. |
| N.S. | Nursing Sister. |
| O.C. | Officer Commanding. |
| O.H.L. | Oberste Heeresleitung, i.e. German Supreme Command. |
| O.M.F.C. | Overseas Military Forces of Canada. |
| O.O. | Operation Order. |
| O.P. | Observation Post or Party. |
| O.R. | Other Ranks. |
| P.C. | Privy Council, or poste de commandement, i.e., headquarters of a field formation. |
| pdr. | pounder. |
| P.F. | Permanent Force (Canadian Militia). |
| Q. | Branch of the Quarter-Master-General. |
| Q.F. | Quick Firing. |
| Q.M.G. | Quarter-Master-General. |
| Q.M.S. | Quartermaster-Sergeant. |
| R.A.P. | Regimental Aid Post. |
| R. & F. | Rank and File. |
| R.B. | Reserve Brigade. (German). |
| R.D. : | Reserve Division. (German). |
| rds. | Rounds. |
| rept. reptd. | Repeat(ed). |
| R.E.R. | Reserve Ersatz Division. (German). |
| Res. | Reserve. |
| Res. of Off. | Reserve of Officers. |
| R.I.R. | Reserve Infantry Regiment. (German). |
| R.M.C. | Royal Military College. |
| R.N. | Royal Navy. |

| | |
|---|---|
| R.N.V.R. | Royal Naval Volunteer Reserve. |
| R.O. | Routine Orders, or Reserve of Officers. |
| R.S.M. | Regimental Sergeant-Major. |
| R.T.O. | Railway Transport Officer. |
| S.A.A. | Small Arms Ammunition. |
| S.C. | Southern Command or Staff Captain. |
| S/Capt. | Staff Captain. |
| Sec. | Section. |
| S.H. | Historical Section of the French General Staff. |
| Sig(s) | Signal(s). |
| S.M. | Sergeant-Major. |
| S.M.L.E. | Short Magazine Lee-Enfield. |
| S.O. | Staff Officer. |
| S.O.O. | Senior Ordnance Officer. |
| S.O.S. | Emergency call for help. |
| S.S.A.C. | Standing Small Arms Committee. |
| T. | Territorial. |
| temp. | temporary. |
| T.F. | Territorial Force. |
| T.M. | Trench Mortar. |
| Vet. | Veterinary. |
| W.E. | War Establishment. |
| W.O. | War Office. U. |

# CANADIAN FORCES

| | |
|---|---|
| CA. or Cdn. Arty. | Canadian Artillery. |
| C.A.D.C. | Canadian Army Dental Corps. |
| C.A.M.C. | Canadian Army Medical Corps. |
| C.A.P.C. | Canadian Army Pay Corps. |
| C.A.S.C. | Canadian Army Service Corps. |
| C.A.V.C. | Canadian Army Veterinary Corps. |
| C.D.A. | Canadian Divisional Artillery. |
| Cdn. Cav. Bde. | Canadian Cavalry Brigade. |
| C.E. | Canadian Engineers. |
| C.F.A. | Canadian Field Artillery. |
| C.G.A. | Canadian Garrison Artillery. |
| C.I.B. | Canadian Infantry Brigade. |
| C.M.M.G. Bde. | Canadian Motor Machine Gun Brigade. |
| C.M.R. Regt. | Canadian Mounted Rifles Regiment. |
| C.M.S.C. | Corps of Military Staff Clerks. |
| C.O.C. | Canadian Ordnance Corps. |
| C.O.T.C. | Canadian Officers' Training Corps. |
| C.P.A.S.C. | Canadian Permanent Army Service |
| Corps. C.P.A.V.C. | Canadian Permanent Army |
| Veterinary Corps. C.P.C. | Canadian Postal |
| Corps. C.S.C. | Canadian Signal Corps. |
| C.T.D. | Canadian Training Depot. |
| C.O.R.C.C. | Canadian Overseas Railway Construction Corps. |
| F.G.H. | Fort Garry Horse. |
| L.S.H.(R.C.) | Lord Strathcona's Horse (Royal Canadians). |
| P.A.M.C. | Permanent Army Medical Corps. |

144

P.P.C.L.I. .................................................................Princess Patricia's Canadian Light Infantry.
R.C.A. .................................................................Royal Canadian Artillery.
R.C.D. .................................................................Royal Canadian Dragoons.
R.C.E. .................................................................Royal Canadian Engineers.
R.C.G.A. .................................................................Royal Canadian Garrison Artillery.
R.C.H.A. .................................................................Royal Canadian Horse Artillery.
R.C.N. .................................................................Royal Canadian Navy.
R.C.R. .................................................................The Royal Canadian Regiment.
R.M.C. .................................................................Royal Military College.
R.N.C.V.R. .................................................................Royal Naval Canadian Volunteer Reserve.
R.N.W.M.P. .................................................................Royal North West Mounted Police.
R.S.A. .................................................................Royal School of Artillery.

# III. BRITISH REGIMENTAL

A.&S.H. .................................................Princess Louise's (Argyll and Sutherland High. larders).
A.S.C. .................................................................Army Service Corps.
Buffs. .................................................................The Buffs (East Kent Regiment).
Ches. or Cheshire .................................................................The Cheshire Regiment.
D.C.L.I. .................................................................The Duke of Cornwall's Light Infantry.
D.L.I. .................................................................The Durham Light Infantry.
E. Kent .................................................................The Buffs (East Kent Regiment).
Essex .................................................................The Essex Regiment.
E. Surrey .................................................................The East Surrey Regiment.
E. York .................................................................The East Yorkshire Regiment.

K.E.H. .................King Edward's Horse (The King's Oversew Do minion Regiment).
K.O.R. Lanc .................................................The King's Own (Royal Lancaster
Regiment). K.O.S.B. .................................................The King's Own Scottish
Borderers. K.O.Y.L.I. .................................................The King's Own Yorkshire
Light Infantry. K.S.L.I. .................................................The King's (Shropshire
Light Infantry). K.R.R.C. .................................................The King's Royal Rifle Corps.
Linc. .................................................................The Lincolnshire Regiment.
9/London(Q.V.R.) .................9th London Regiment (Queen, Victoria's Rifles).
L'pool .................................................................The King's (Liverpool Regiment).
Middx. .................................................The Duke of Cambridge's Own (Middlesex Regiment).
Mon. .................................................................The Monmouthshire Regiment.
N.Fus. .................................................................The Northumberland Fusiliers.
R.A. .................................................................Royal Artillery.
R.A.M.C. .................................................................Royal Army Medical Corps.
R.E. .................................................................Royal Engineers.
R.F.A. .................................................................Royal Field Artillery.
R.F.C. .................................................................Royal Flying Corps.
R. Fusiliers .................................................The Royal Fusiliers (City of London Regiment).
R.G.A. .................................................................Royal Garrison Artillery.
Rifle Bde. .................................................The Rifle Brigade (The Prince Consort's
Own). R. Ir. Fus. .................................................Princess Victoria's (Royal Irish Fusiliers).
R. Ir. Rif. .................................................................The Royal Irish Rifles.
R.N.A.S. .................................................................Royal Naval Air Service.
R. Scots .................................................................The Royal Scots (Lothian Regiment). R.
West Kent .................................................The Queen's Own (Royal West Kent Regiment)

Highrs. ...................................................................The Seaforth Highlanders (Ross-shire Buffs, The Duke of Albany's)

Shrops. L.I. ...................................................................The King's (Shropshire Light Infantry).

Suff. ...................................................................The Suffolk Regiment.

Welch...................................................................The Welch Regiment.

Wilts. ...................................................................The Duke of Edinburgh's (Wiltshire Regiment).

W. Rid. ...................................................................The Duke of Wellington's (West Riding Regiment).

Y.&L. or York & Lanc. ...................................................................The York and Lancaster Regiment.

York ...................................................................Alexandra, Princess of Wales's Own (Yorkshire Regiment).

# ABOUT THE AUTHOR

William H. Graham was born in Sydney, Nova Scotia in 1940 and continued his life in Ontario in 1985. He is a husband to Shirley, a father, grandfather and great grandfather who has had an interesting life doing many different things.

As he gets older, the things that become increasingly important in his life are: religion, family and groups he and Shirley can support to help those in need.

William and Shirley currently live in Mississauga, Ontario.

Manufactured by Amazon.ca
Bolton, ON

29709453R00090